POEMS OF ROBERT BURNS

POEMS OF
ROBERT BURNS

Illustrated by
W. Russell Flint and R. Purves Flint

GRAMERCY BOOKS
New York • Avenel

Introduction and compilation
Copyright © 1994 by Outlet Book Company, Inc.

Published by Gramercy Books,
distributed by Outlet Book Company, Inc.
a Random House Company,
40 Engelhard Avenue
Avenel, New Jersey 07001

Random House
New York • Toronto • London • Sydney • Auckland

Designed by Melissa Ring

Printed and bound in Singapore

Library of Congress Cataloging-in-Publication Data
Burns, Robert, 1759-1796.
[Poems]
Poems of Robert Burns / illustrated by W. Russell Flint
and R. Purves Flint
p. cm.
ISBN 0-517-10063-0
I. Title.
PR4303 1994
821'.6—dc20   93-42544
                                       CIP
10 9 8 7 6 5 4 3 2 1

CONTENTS

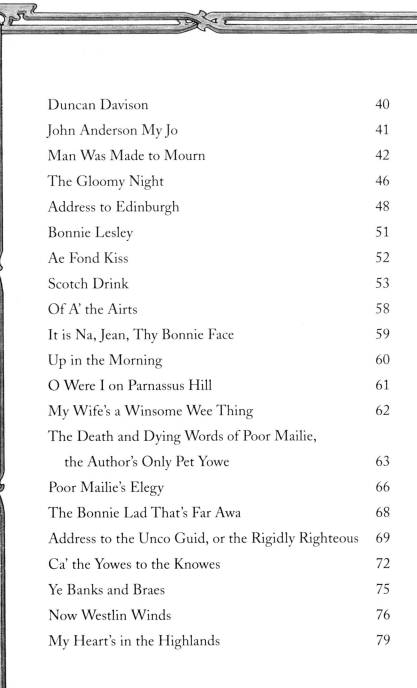

INTRODUCTION

Robert Burns, the Scottish national bard, is one of the best-loved poets of all time. He was also a brilliant satirist who rebelled against the social order of his day and against any political or religious thought that condoned inhumanity.

Burns was born on January 25, 1759 in a cotter's cottage in Alloway near Ayr, the eldest son of a tenant farmer. The family was poor and moved from one farm to another, but Burns managed to pick up bits of education. Although he was forced to work hard throughout his boyhood he was a great reader, always carrying a few small books in his pocket so he could read while he ate or when he had a few spare minutes in the fields. A favorite book was a collection of songs, of which he wrote, "I pored over them, driving my cart or walking to labour, song by song, verse by verse, carefully noting the true, the tender, sublime or fustian."

He began to write poetry himself. Among his early poems was "Death of Poor Mailie." When Burns was twenty-five, his father died and he and his brother Gilbert moved the family to Mossgiel where, for four years, they unsuccessfully farmed more than a hundred acres. During these years Burns wrote some of his best poems including "The Cotter's Saturday Night," "To a Mouse," and "To a Daisy," as well as some of his most popular songs.

Meanwhile, he had met and fallen in love with Jean Armour, but her father, a master mason, disapproved of the match and would not permit Jean to marry him. In 1786, Burns gave up his courtship and accepted a job as a bookkeeper on a plantation in Jamaica. To obtain money for his passage he arranged for the publication of his first collection of poems.

The book met with great success. "With his poems," wrote Robert Heron, "old and young, grave and gay, learned and ignorant, were alike transported." Although the first edition brought Burns little money, he abandoned his West Indian venture and moved to Edinburgh where the literary elite welcomed, admired, and lionized him. From the second edition of the book, which was published in 1787, Burns received £400— more money than he had ever had in his life. He took two inspiring trips; one through the border towns of Scotland into England, the other through the East Highlands.

In 1788, Burns moved to a new farm at Ellislan on the Mirth, married his beloved Jean, and lost the little money he had left. He continued to write, among other pieces "Auld Lang Syne" and "Tam o' Shanter," and he composed and restored the words to a wealth of Scottish folk tunes.

In the last years of his life Burns was no longer accepted in polite society because of his revolutionary opinions. He became weak from rheumatic heart disease, the result of too much physical exertion on an inadequate diet when he was young. He died on July 25th, 1796. He was only thirty-seven years old.

GAIL HARVEY

New York
1994

MARY MORISON

O MARY, at thy window be,
 It is the wish'd, the trysted hour!
Those smiles and glances let me see,
 That make the miser's treasure poor:
How blythely wad I bide the stoure,
 A weary slave frae sun to sun,
Could I the rich reward secure,
 The lovely Mary Morison.

Yestreen, when to the trembling string
 The dance gaed thro' the lighted ha',
To thee my fancy took its wing,
 I sat, but neither heard nor saw:
Tho' this was fair, and that was braw,
 And yon the toast of a' the town,
I sigh'd, and said amang them a',
 'Ye are na Mary Morison.'

O Mary, canst thou wreck his peace,
 Wha for thy sake wad gladly die?
Or canst thou break that heart of his,
 Whase only faut is loving thee?

TO A MOUSE, ON TURNING HER UP IN HER NEST WITH THE PLOUGH, NOVEMBER, 1785

Wee, sleekit, cow'rin', tim'rous beastie,
O what a panic 's in thy breastie !
Thou need na start awa sae hasty,
      Wi' bickering brattle !
I wad be laith to rin an' chase thee
      Wi' murd'ring pattle !

I'm truly sorry man's dominion
Has broken Nature's social union,
An' justifies that ill opinion
      Which makes thee startle
At me, thy poor earth-born companion,
      An' fellow-mortal !

I doubt na, whiles, but thou may thieve ;
What then ? poor beastie, thou maun live !
A daimen-icker in a thrave
      'S a sma' request :
I'll get a blessin' wi' the lave,
      And never miss 't !

Thy wee bit housie, too, in ruin !
Its silly wa's the win's are strewin' !
An' naething, now, to big a new ane,
      O' foggage green !
An' bleak December's winds ensuin',
      Baith snell an' keen !

Thou saw the fields laid bare and waste,
An' weary winter comin' fast,
An' cozie here, beneath the blast,
        Thou thought to dwell,
Till crash ! the cruel coulter past
        Out-thro' thy cell.

That wee bit heap o' leaves an' stibble
Has cost thee mony a weary nibble !
Now thou 's turn'd out, for a' thy trouble,
        But house or hald,
To thole the winter's sleety dribble,
        An' cranreuch cauld !

But, Mousie, thou art no thy lane,
In proving foresight may be vain :
The best laid schemes o' mice an' men
        Gang aft a-gley,
An' lea'e us nought but grief an' pain
        For promis'd joy.

Still thou art blest compar'd wi' me !
The present only toucheth thee :
But oh ! I backward cast my e'e
        On prospects drear !
An' forward tho' I canna see,
        I guess an' fear !

GO FETCH TO ME A PINT O' WINE

Go fetch to me a pint o' wine,
   An' fill it in a silver tassie;
That I may drink, before I go,
   A service to my bonnie lassie.
The boat rocks at the pier o' Leith,
   Fu' loud the wind blaws frae the ferry,
The ship rides by the Berwick-law,
   And I maun leave my bonnie Mary.

The trumpets sound, the banners fly,
   The glittering spears are rankèd ready;
The shouts o' war are heard afar,
   The battle closes thick and bloody;
But it's no the roar o' sea or shore
   Wad mak me langer wish to tarry;
Nor shout o' war that's heard afar,
   It's leaving thee, my bonnie Mary.

MY LOVE IS LIKE A RED RED ROSE

My love is like a red red rose
　That's newly sprung in June:
My love is like the melodie
　That's sweetly play'd in tune.

So fair art thou, my bonnie lass,
　So deep in love am I:
And I will love thee still, my dear,
　Till a' the seas gang dry.

Till a' the seas gang dry, my dear,
　And the rocks melt wi' the sun:
And I will love thee still, my dear,
　While the sands o' life shall run.

And fare thee weel, my only love,
　And fare thee weel awhile!
And I will come again, my love,
　Tho' it were ten thousand mile.

BLYTHE AND MERRY

By Ochtertyre there grows the aik,
  On Yarrow banks the birken shaw;
But Phemie was a bonnier lass
  Than braes o' Yarrow ever saw.

    Blythe, blythe and merry was she,
      Blythe was she but and ben:
    Blythe by the banks of Earn,
      And blythe in Glenturit glen.

Her looks were like a flower in May,
  Her smile was like a simmer morn;
She trippèd by the banks of Earn
  As light's a bird upon a thorn.

Her bonnie face it was as meek
  As ony lamb's upon a lea;
The evening sun was ne'er sae sweet
  As was the blink o' Phemie's e'e.

The Highland hills I've wander'd wide,
  And o'er the Lowlands I hae been;
But Phemie was the blythest lass
  That ever trod the dewy green.

AFTON WATER

Flow gently, sweet Afton, among thy green braes,
Flow gently, I'll sing thee a song in thy praise ;
My Mary's asleep by thy murmuring stream,
Flow gently, sweet Afton, disturb not her dream.

Thou stock-dove whose echo resounds thro' the glen,
Ye wild whistling blackbirds in yon thorny den,
Thou green-crested lapwing, thy screaming forbear,
I charge you disturb not my slumbering fair.

How lofty, sweet Afton, thy neighbouring hills,
Far mark'd with the courses of clear winding rills ;
There daily I wander as noon rises high,
My flocks and my Mary's sweet cot in my eye.

How pleasant thy banks and green valleys below,
Where wild in the woodlands the primroses blow ;
There oft as mild ev'ning weeps over the lea,
The sweet-scented birk shades my Mary and me.

Thy crystal stream, Afton, how lovely it glides,
And winds by the cot where my Mary resides ;
How wanton thy waters her snowy feet lave,
As gathering sweet flow'rets she stems thy clear wave.

Flow gently, sweet Afton, among thy green braes,
Flow gently, sweet river, the theme of my lays ;
My Mary's asleep by thy murmuring stream,
Flow gently, sweet Afton, disturb not her dream.

WHEN I THINK ON THE HAPPY DAYS

WHEN I think on the happy days
    I spent wi' you, my dearie ;
And now what lands between us lie,
    How can I be but eerie !

How slow ye move, ye heavy hours,
    As ye were wae and weary !
It was na sae ye glinted by
    When I was wi' my dearie.

IT WAS A' FOR OUR RIGHTFU' KING

It was a' for our rightfu' King,
   We left fair Scotland's strand ;
It was a' for our rightfu' King,
   We e'er saw Irish land,
         My dear,
   We e'er saw Irish land.

Now a' is done that men can do,
   And a' is done in vain ;
My love and native land farewell,
   For I maun cross the main,
         My dear,
   For I maun cross the main.

He turn'd him right and round about
   Upon the Irish shore ;
And gae his bridle-reins a shake,
   With adieu for evermore,
         My dear,
   Adieu for evermore.

The sodger from the wars returns,
  The sailor frae the main ;
But I hae parted frae my love,
  Never to meet again,
              My dear,
  Never to meet again.

When day is gane, and night is come,
  And a' folk boune to sleep,
I think on him that's far awa',
  The lee-lang night, and weep,
              My dear,
  The lee-lang night, and weep.

TO MARY IN HEAVEN

Thou lingering star, with lessening ray,
　　Thou lov'st to greet the early morn,
Again thou usherest in the day
　　My Mary from my soul was torn.
O Mary! dear departed shade!
　　Where is thy place of blissful rest?
Seest thou thy lover lowly laid?
　　Hear'st thou the groans that rend his breast?

That sacred hour can I forget?
　　Can I forget the hallow'd grove,
Where by the winding Ayr we met,
　　To live one day of parting love?
Eternity will not efface
　　Those records dear of transports past;
Thy image at our last embrace—
　　Ah! little thought we 'twas our last!

Ayr gurgling kiss'd his pebbled shore,
　　O'erhung with wild woods, thickening green;
The fragrant birch, and hawthorn hoar,
　　Twin'd amorous round the raptur'd scene.

The flowers sprang wanton to be prest,
　　The birds sang love on ev'ry spray,
Till too too soon, the glowing west
　　Proclaim'd the speed of wingèd day.

Still o'er these scenes my memory wakes,
　　And fondly broods with miser care!
Time but the impression deeper makes,
　　As streams their channels deeper wear.
My Mary, dear departed shade!
　　Where is thy blissful place of rest?
Seest thou thy lover lowly laid?
　　Hear'st thou the groans that rend his breast?

LOGAN BRAES

O LOGAN, sweetly didst thou glide
That day I was my Willie's bride ;
And years sinsyne hae o'er us run,
Like Logan to the simmer sun.
But now thy flow'ry banks appear
Like drumlie winter, dark and drear,
While my dear lad maun face his faes,
Far, far frae me and Logan Braes.

Again the merry month o' May
Has made our hills and valleys gay ;
The birds rejoice in leafy bowers,
The bees hum round the breathing flowers ;
Blithe morning lifts his rosy eye,
And evening's tears are tears of joy :
My soul, delightless, a' surveys,
While Willie's far frae Logan Braes.

Within yon milk-white hawthorn bush,
Amang her nestlings, sits the thrush ;
Her faithfu' mate will share her toil,
Or wi' his song her cares beguile :
But I wi' my sweet nurslings here,
Nae mate to help, nae mate to cheer,
Pass widow'd nights and joyless days,
While Willie's far frae Logan Braes.

O wae upon you, men o' state,
That brethren rouse to deadly hate !
As ye mak mony a fond heart mourn,
Sae may it on your heads return !
How can your flinty hearts enjoy
The widow's tears, the orphan's cry ?
But soon may peace bring happy days,
And Willie hame to Logan Braes !

ON THE BATTLE OF SHERIFFMUIR

BETWEEN THE DUKE OF ARGYLE AND THE EARL OF MAR

'O CAM ye here the fight to shun,
    Or herd the sheep wi' me, man ?
Or were you at the Sherra-muir,
    And did the battle see, man ?'
I saw the battle, sair and teugh,
And reeking-red ran mony a sheugh ;
My heart, for fear, gae sough for sough,
To hear the thuds, and see the cluds
O' clans frae woods, in tartan duds,
    Wha glaum'd at kingdoms three, man.

The red-coat lads, wi' black cockades,
    To meet them were na slaw, man ;
They rush'd and push'd, and blude out-gush'd,
    And mony a bouk did fa', man :
The great Argyle led on his files,
I wat they glancèd twenty miles :
They hough'd the clans like nine-pin kyles,
They hack'd and hash'd, while broadswords clash'd,
And thro' they dash'd, and hew'd and smash'd,
    Till fey men died awa, man.

But had you seen the philibegs,
    And skyrin tartan trews, man,
When in the teeth they dar'd our whigs,
    And covenant true blues, man ;
In lines extended lang and large,
When baig'nets overpower'd the targe,
And thousands hasten'd to the charge,
Wi' Highland wrath they frae the sheath
Drew blades o' death, till, out of breath,
    They fled like frighted doos, man.

'O how deil, Tam, can that be true ?
　　The chase gaed frae the north, man :
I saw mysel, they did pursue
　　The horsemen back to Forth, man ;
And at Dumblane, in my ain sight,
They took the brig wi' a' their might,
And straught to Stirling wing'd their flight ;
But, cursèd lot ! the gates were shut,
And mony a huntit, poor red-coat,
　　For fear amaist did swarf, man.'

My sister Kate cam up the gate
　　Wi' crowdie unto me, man ;
She swore she saw some rebels run
　　Frae Perth unto Dundee, man :
Their left-hand general had nae skill,
The Angus lads had nae guid-will,
That day their neibors' blood to spill ;
For fear, by foes, that they should lose
Their cogs o' brose, they scared at blows,
　　And hameward fast did flee, man.

They've lost some gallant gentlemen
　　Amang the Highland clans, man ;
I fear my lord Panmure is slain,
　　Or fallen in whiggish hands, man :
Now wad ye sing this double fight,
Some fell for wrang, and some for right ;
But mony bade the world guid-night ;
Then ye may tell, how pell and mell,
By red claymores, and muskets' knell,
Wi' dying yell, the tories fell,
　　And whigs to hell did flee, man.

THE RIGS O' BARLEY

It was upon a Lammas night,
  When corn rigs are bonnie,
Beneath the moon's unclouded light
  I held awa to Annie :
The time flew by wi' tentless heed,
  Till 'tween the late and early,
Wi' sma' persuasion she agreed
  To see me thro' the barley.

The sky was blue, the wind was still,
  The moon was shining clearly ;
I set her down wi' right good will
  Amang the rigs o' barley ;
I kent her heart was a' my ain ;
  I loved her most sincerely ;
I kissed her owre and owre again
  Amang the rigs o' barley.

I locked her in my fond embrace ;
  Her heart was beating rarely ;
My blessings on that happy place,
  Amang the rigs o' barley !
But by the moon and stars so bright,
  That shone that hour so clearly,
She aye shall bless that happy night
  Amang the rigs o' barley.

I hae been blythe wi' comrades dear ;
　I hae been merry drinking ;
I hae been joyfu' gatherin' gear ;
　I hae been happy thinking :
But a' the pleasures e'er I saw,
　Tho' three times doubled fairly,
That happy night was worth them a',
　Amang the rigs o' barley.

　　Corn rigs, an' barley rigs,
　　　An' corn rigs are bonnie :
　　I'll ne'er forget that happy night,
　　　Amang the rigs wi' Annie.

A WINTER NIGHT

When biting Boreas, fell and dour,
Sharp shivers thro' the leafless bow'r ;
When Phœbus gies a short-liv'd glow'r,
      Far south the lift,
Dim-dark'ning thro' the flaky show'r
      Or whirling drift ;

Ae night the storm the steeples rocked,
Poor Labour sweet in sleep was locked,
While burns, wi' snawy wreaths up-choked,
      Wild-eddying swirl,
Or, thro' the mining outlet bocked,
      Down headlong hurl ;

List'ning the doors an' winnocks rattle,
I thought me on the ourie cattle,
Or silly sheep, wha bide this brattle
      O' winter war,
And thro' the drift, deep-lairing, sprattle
      Beneath a scar.

Ilk happing bird, wee, helpless thing !
That, in the merry months o' spring,
Delighted me to hear thee sing,
      What comes o' thee ?
Whare wilt thou cow'r thy chittering wing,
      An' close thy e'e ?

Ev'n you, on murdering errands toil'd,
Lone from your savage homes exil'd,—
The blood-stained roost and sheep-cote spoil'd
　　　My heart forgets,
While pitiless the tempest wild
　　　Sore on you beats.

Now Phœbe, in her midnight reign,
Dark muffl'd, view'd the dreary plain ;
Still crowding thoughts, a pensive train,
　　　Rose in my soul,
When on my ear this plaintive strain,
　　　Slow, solemn, stole :—

' Blow, blow, ye winds, with heavier gust !
And freeze, thou bitter-biting frost !
Descend, ye chilly smothering snows !
Not all your rage, as now united, shows
　　More hard unkindness unrelenting,
　　Vengeful malice unrepenting,
Than heav'n-illumin'd man on brother man bestows !
　　See stern Oppression's iron grip,
　　　Or mad Ambition's gory hand,
　　Sending, like blood-hounds from the slip,
　　　Woe, want, and murder o'er a land !

　　Ev'n in the peaceful rural vale,
　　Truth, weeping, tells the mournful tale
How pamper'd Luxury, Flatt'ry by her side,
　　The parasite empoisoning her ear,
　　With all the servile wretches in the rear,

Looks o'er proud property, extended wide ;
    And eyes the simple rustic hind,
        Whose toil upholds the glitt'ring show,
    A creature of another kind,
    Some coarser substance, unrefin'd,
Plac'd for her lordly use thus far, thus vile, below.

    Where, where is Love's fond, tender throe,
    With lordly Honour's lofty brow,
        The pow'rs you proudly own ?
    Is there, beneath Love's noble name,
    Can harbour, dark, the selfish aim
        To bless himself alone ?
    Mark maiden-innocence a prey
        To love-pretending snares ;
    This boasted honour turns away,
    Shunning soft pity's rising sway,
Regardless of the tears, and unavailing pray'rs !
    Perhaps this hour, in mis'ry's squalid nest,
    She strains your infant to her joyless breast,
And with a mother's fears shrinks at the rocking blast !

    Oh ye ! who, sunk in beds of down,
Feel not a want but what yourselves create,
Think, for a moment, on his wretched fate,
    Whom friends and fortune quite disown !
Ill satisfied keen nature's clam'rous call,
    Stretch'd on his straw he lays himself to sleep,

While thro' the ragged roof and chinky wall,
Chill o'er his slumbers piles the drifty heap !
Think on the dungeon's grim confine,

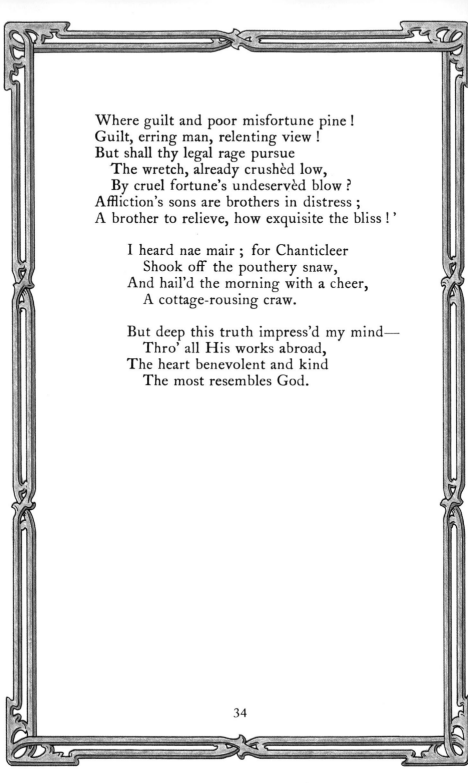

Where guilt and poor misfortune pine !
Guilt, erring man, relenting view !
But shall thy legal rage pursue
   The wretch, already crushèd low,
   By cruel fortune's undeservèd blow ?
Affliction's sons are brothers in distress ;
A brother to relieve, how exquisite the bliss ! '

   I heard nae mair ; for Chanticleer
      Shook off the pouthery snaw,
   And hail'd the morning with a cheer,
      A cottage-rousing craw.

   But deep this truth impress'd my mind—
      Thro' all His works abroad,
   The heart benevolent and kind
      The most resembles God.

THO' CRUEL FATE

Tho' cruel fate should bid us part,
　　Wide as the pole and line ;
Her dear idea round my heart
　　Should tenderly entwine.

Tho' mountains rise and deserts howl,
　　And oceans roar between ;
Yet, dearer than my deathless soul,
　　I still would love my Jean.

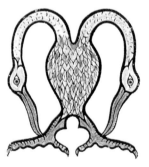

TO A MOUNTAIN DAISY

ON TURNING ONE DOWN WITH THE PLOUGH
IN APRIL, 1786

Wee modest crimson-tippèd flow'r,
Thou 's met me in an evil hour;
For I maun crush amang the stoure
       Thy slender stem :
To spare thee now is past my pow'r,
       Thou bonnie gem.

Alas ! it's no thy neibor sweet,
The bonnie lark, companion meet,
Bending thee 'mang the dewy weet
       Wi' spreckl'd breast,
When upward springing, blythe to greet
       The purpling east.

Cauld blew the bitter-biting north
Upon thy early humble birth ;
Yet cheerfully thou glinted forth
       Amid the storm,
Scarce rear'd above the parent-earth
       Thy tender form.

The flaunting flow'rs our gardens yield
High shelt'ring woods and wa's maun shield,
But thou, beneath the random bield
       O' clod or stane,
Adorns the histie stibble-field,
       Unseen, alane.

There, in thy scanty mantle clad,
Thy snawy bosom sun-ward spread,
Thou lifts thy unassuming head
                    In humble guise;
But now the share uptears thy bed,
                    And low thou lies!

Such is the fate of artless maid,
Sweet flow'ret of the rural shade,
By love's simplicity betray'd,
                    And guileless trust,
Till she like thee, all soil'd, is laid
                    Low i' the dust.

Such is the fate of simple bard,
On life's rough ocean luckless starr'd:
Unskilful he to note the card
                    Of prudent lore,
Till billows rage, and gales blow hard,
                    And whelm him o'er!

Such fate to suffering worth is giv'n,
Who long with wants and woes has striv'n,
By human pride or cunning driv'n
                    To mis'ry's brink,
Till wrench'd of ev'ry stay but Heav'n,
                    He, ruin'd, sink!

Ev'n thou who mourn'st the Daisy's fate,
That fate is thine—no distant date;
Stern Ruin's ploughshare drives elate
                    Full on thy bloom,
Till crush'd beneath the furrow's weight
                    Shall be thy doom!

THOUGHTS IN WINTER

THE wintry wast extends his blast,
  And hail and rain does blaw ;
Or the stormy north sends driving forth
  The blinding sleet and snaw :
While, tumbling brown, the burn comes down,
  And roars frae bank to brae :
And bird and beast in covert rest,
  And pass the heartless day.

'The sweeping blast, the sky o'ercast,'
  The joyless winter-day,
Let others fear, to me more dear
  Than all the pride of May :
The tempest's howl, it soothes my soul,
  My griefs it seems to join ;
The leafless trees my fancy please,
  Their fate resembles mine !

Thou Pow'r Supreme, whose mighty scheme
  These woes of mine fulfil,
Here, firm, I rest,—they must be best,
  Because they are Thy will !
Then all I want (Oh ! do thou grant
  This one request of mine !)
Since to enjoy thou dost deny,
  Assist me to resign.

DUNCAN DAVISON

There was a lass, they ca'd her Meg,
 And she held o'er the moors to spin ;
There was a lad that follow'd her,
 They ca'd him Duncan Davison.
The moor was driegh, and Meg was skiegh,
 Her favour Duncan could na win ;
For wi' the rock she wad him knock,
 And ay she shook the temper-pin.

As o'er the moor they lightly foor,
 A burn was clear, a glen was green,
Upon the banks they eased their shanks,
 And aye she set the wheel between :
But Duncan swore a haly aith,
 That Meg should be a bride the morn ;
Then Meg took up her spinnin' graith,
 And flung them a' out o'er the burn.

We'll big a house—a wee, wee house,
 And we will live like King and Queen,
Sae blythe and merry we will be
 When ye set by the wheel at e'en.
A man may drink and no be drunk ;
 A man may fight and no be slain ;
A man may kiss a bonnie lass,
 And aye be welcome back again.

JOHN ANDERSON MY JO

JOHN ANDERSON my jo, John,
　　When we were first acquent,
Your locks were like the raven,
　　Your bonnie brow was brent ;
But now your brow is beld, John,
　　Your locks are like the snow ;
But blessings on your frosty pow,
　　John Anderson, my jo.

John Anderson my jo, John,
　　We clamb the hill thegither ;
And mony a canty day, John,
　　We've had wi' ane anither :
Now we maun totter down, John,
　　And hand in hand we'll go,
And sleep thegither at the foot,
　　John Anderson, my jo.

MAN WAS MADE TO MOURN

WHEN chill November's surly blast
  Made fields and forests bare,
One ev'ning as I wander'd forth
  Along the banks of Ayr,
I spied a man, whose agèd step
  Seem'd weary, worn with care ;
His face was furrow'd o'er with years,
  And hoary was his hair.

'Young stranger, whither wand'rest thou ?'
  Began the rev'rend sage ;
'Does thirst of wealth thy step constrain,
  Or youthful pleasure's rage ?
Or, haply, prest with cares and woes,
  Too soon thou hast began
To wander forth with me to mourn
  The miseries of man.

'The sun that overhangs yon moors,
  Out-spreading far and wide,
Where hundreds labour to support
  A haughty lordling's pride—
I've seen yon weary winter-sun
  Twice forty times return,
And ev'ry time has added proofs
  That man was made to mourn.

'O man ! while in thy early years,
    How prodigal of time !
Mis-spending all thy precious hours,
    Thy glorious youthful prime !
Alternate follies take the sway ;
    Licentious passions burn ;
Which tenfold force give nature's law,
    That man was made to mourn.

'Look not alone on youthful prime,
    Or manhood's active might ;
Man then is useful to his kind,
    Supported is his right ;
But see him on the edge of life,
    With cares and sorrows worn,
Then age and want, oh ! ill-match'd pair !
    Show man was made to mourn.

'A few seem favourites of fate,
    In pleasure's lap carest ;
Yet think not all the rich and great
    Are likewise truly blest.
But oh ! what crowds in ev'ry land
    All wretched and forlorn,
Thro' weary life this lesson learn—
    That man was made to mourn.

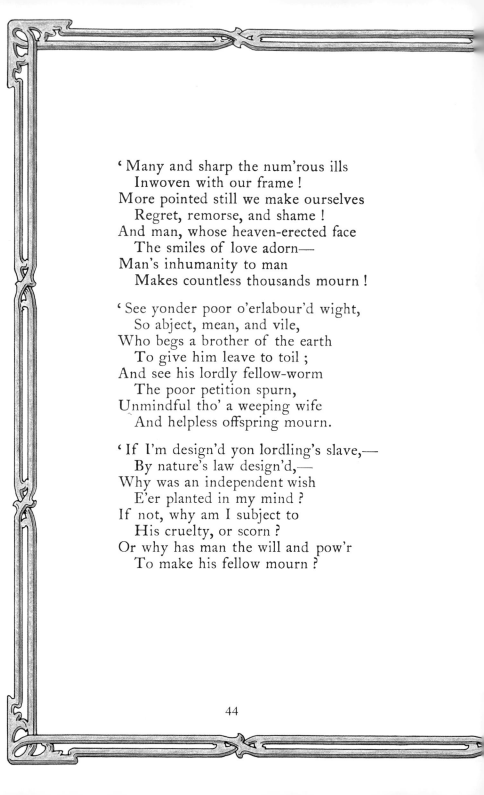

‘ Many and sharp the num’rous ills
    Inwoven with our frame !
More pointed still we make ourselves
    Regret, remorse, and shame !
And man, whose heaven-erected face
    The smiles of love adorn—
Man’s inhumanity to man
    Makes countless thousands mourn !

‘ See yonder poor o’erlabour’d wight,
    So abject, mean, and vile,
Who begs a brother of the earth
    To give him leave to toil ;
And see his lordly fellow-worm
    The poor petition spurn,
Unmindful tho’ a weeping wife
    And helpless offspring mourn.

‘ If I’m design’d yon lordling’s slave,—
    By nature’s law design’d,—
Why was an independent wish
    E’er planted in my mind ?
If not, why am I subject to
    His cruelty, or scorn ?
Or why has man the will and pow’r
    To make his fellow mourn ?

'Yet let not this too much, my son,
    Disturb thy youthful breast ;
This partial view of human-kind
    Is surely not the last !
The poor oppressèd honest man
    Had never sure been born
Had there not been some recompense
    To comfort those that mourn !

'O Death, the poor man's dearest friend,
    The kindest and the best !
Welcome the hour my agèd limbs
    Are laid with thee at rest !
The great, the wealthy, fear thy blow,
    From pomp and pleasure torn ;
But oh ; a blest relief to those
    That weary-laden mourn.'

THE GLOOMY NIGHT

THE gloomy night is gathering fast,
Loud roars the wild inconstant blast,
Yon murky cloud is foul with rain,
I see it driving o'er the plain ;
The hunter now has left the moor,
The scatter'd coveys meet secure,
While here I wander, prest with care,
Along the lonely banks of Ayr.

The Autumn mourns her ripening corn
By early Winter's ravage torn ;
Across her placid azure sky,
She sees the scowling tempest fly :
Chill runs my blood to hear it rave,
I think upon the stormy wave,
Where many a danger I must dare,
Far from the bonnie banks of Ayr.

'Tis not the surging billow's roar,
'Tis not that fatal, deadly shore ;
Tho' death in ev'ry shape appear,
The wretched have no more to fear :
But round my heart the ties are bound,
That heart transpierc'd with many a wound :
These bleed afresh, those ties I tear,
To leave the bonnie banks of Ayr.

Farewell, old Coila's hills and dales,
Her heathy moors and winding vales ;
The scenes where wretched fancy roves,
Pursuing past unhappy loves !
Farewell, my friends !   Farewell, my foes !
My peace with these, my love with those ;
The bursting tears my heart declare,
Farewell, the bonnie banks of Ayr !

ADDRESS TO EDINBURGH

EDINA ! Scotia's darling seat,
   All hail thy palaces and tow'rs,
Where once beneath a monarch's feet
   Sat Legislation's sov'reign pow'rs.
   From marking wildly-scatter'd flow'rs,
As on the banks of Ayr I stray'd,
   And singing lone the ling'ring hours,
I shelter in thy honour'd shade.

Here Wealth still swells the golden tide,
   As busy trade his labours plies ;
There Architecture's noble pride
   Bids elegance and splendour rise ;
   Here Justice, from her native skies,
High wields her balance and her rod ;
   There Learning, with his eagle eyes,
Seeks Science in her coy abode.

Thy sons, Edina, social, kind,
   With open arms the stranger hail ;
Their views enlarg'd, their lib'ral mind,
   Above the narrow rural vale ;
   Attentive still to sorrow's wail,
Or modest merit's silent claim :
   And never may their sources fail !
And never envy blot their name !

Thy daughters bright thy walks adorn,
  Gay as the gilded summer sky,
Sweet as the dewy milk-white thorn,
  Dear as the raptur'd thrill of joy.
  Fair Burnet strikes th' adoring eye,
Heaven's beauties on my fancy shine;
  I see the Sire of Love on high,
And own his work indeed divine!

There watching high the least alarms,
  Thy rough rude fortress gleams afar;
Like some bold veteran, gray in arms,
  And mark'd with many a seamy scar:
  The pond'rous wall and massy bar,
Grim-rising o'er the rugged rock,
  Have oft withstood assailing war,
And oft repell'd th' invader's shock.

With awe-struck thought, and pitying tears,
  I view that noble stately dome,
Where Scotia's kings of other years,
  Fam'd heroes, had their royal home;
  Alas, how chang'd the times to come!
Their royal name low in the dust,
  Their hapless race wild-wand'ring roam;
Tho' rigid law cries out 'twas just!

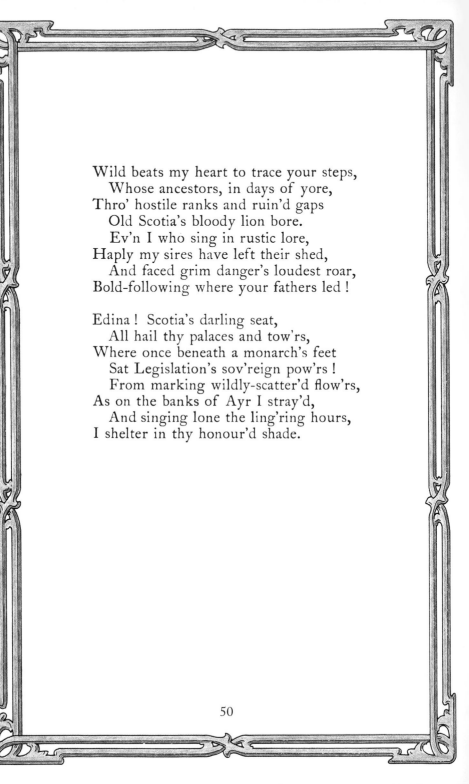

Wild beats my heart to trace your steps,
  Whose ancestors, in days of yore,
Thro' hostile ranks and ruin'd gaps
  Old Scotia's bloody lion bore.
    Ev'n I who sing in rustic lore,
Haply my sires have left their shed,
  And faced grim danger's loudest roar,
Bold-following where your fathers led !

Edina ! Scotia's darling seat,
  All hail thy palaces and tow'rs,
Where once beneath a monarch's feet
  Sat Legislation's sov'reign pow'rs !
    From marking wildly-scatter'd flow'rs,
As on the banks of Ayr I stray'd,
  And singing lone the ling'ring hours,
I shelter in thy honour'd shade.

BONNIE LESLEY

O saw ye bonnie Lesley
   As she gaed o'er the border?
She's gane, like Alexander,
   To spread her conquests farther.

To see her is to love her,
   And love but her for ever;
For Nature made her what she is,
   And never made anither!

Thou art a queen, fair Lesley,
   Thy subjects we, before thee:
Thou art divine, fair Lesley,
   The hearts o' men adore thee.

The Deil he could na scaith thee,
   Or aught that wad belang thee;
He'd look into thy bonnie face,
   And say, 'I canna wrang thee.'

The Powers aboon will tent thee;
   Misfortune sha'na steer thee;
Thou'rt like themselves sae lovely,
   That ill they'll ne'er let near thee.

Return again, fair Lesley,
   Return to Caledonie!
That we may brag we hae a lass
   There's nane again sae bonnie.

AE FOND KISS

Ae fond kiss, and then we sever !
Ae fareweel, alas, for ever !
Deep in heart-wrung tears I'll pledge thee,
Warring sighs and groans I'll wage thee.
Who shall say that fortune grieves him
While the star of hope she leaves him ?
Me, nae cheerfu' twinkle lights me,
Dark despair around benights me.

I'll ne'er blame my partial fancy,
Naething could resist my Nancy ;
But to see her was to love her,
Love but her, and love for ever.
Had we never lov'd sae kindly,
Had we never lov'd sae blindly,
Never met—or never parted,
We had ne'er been broken-hearted.

Fare thee weel, thou first and fairest !
Fare thee weel, thou best and dearest !
Thine be ilka joy and treasure,
Peace, enjoyment, love, and pleasure.
Ae fond kiss, and then we sever ;
Ae fareweel, alas, for ever ;
Deep in heart-wrung tears I'll pledge thee,
Warring sighs and groans I'll wage thee.

SCOTCH DRINK

Gie him strong drink, until he wink,
That's sinking in despair ;
An' liquor guid to fire his bluid,
That's prest wi' grief an' care ;
There let him bouse, an' deep carouse,
Wi' bumpers flowing o'er,
Till he forgets his loves or debts,
An' minds his griefs no more.

SOLOMON (Proverbs xxxi. 6, 7).

LET other Poets raise a fracas
'Bout vines, an' wines, an' drucken Bacchus,
An' crabbèd names an' stories wrack us,
　　　　An' grate our lug ;
I sing the juice Scotch bear can mak us,
　　　　In glass or jug.

O thou, my Muse ! guid auld Scotch Drink,
Whether thro' wimplin worms thou jink,
Or, richly brown, ream owre the brink,
　　　　In glorious faem,
Inspire me, till I lisp an' wink,
　　　　To sing thy name !

Let husky wheat the haughs adorn,
An' aits set up their awnie horn,
An' pease an' beans at een or morn,
　　　　Perfume the plain ;
Leeze me on thee, John Barleycorn,
　　　　Thou King o' grain !

On thee aft Scotland chows her cood,
In souple scones, the wale o' food !
Or tumblin' in the boiling flood
　　　　Wi' kail an' beef ;
But when thou pours thy strong heart's blood,
　　　　There thou shines chief.

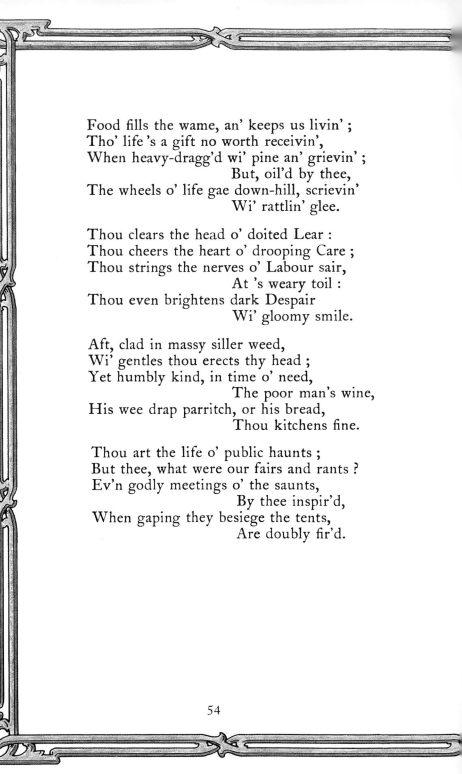

Food fills the wame, an' keeps us livin';
Tho' life 's a gift no worth receivin',
When heavy-dragg'd wi' pine an' grievin';
        But, oil'd by thee,
The wheels o' life gae down-hill, scrievin'
        Wi' rattlin' glee.

Thou clears the head o' doited Lear :
Thou cheers the heart o' drooping Care ;
Thou strings the nerves o' Labour sair,
        At 's weary toil :
Thou even brightens dark Despair
        Wi' gloomy smile.

Aft, clad in massy siller weed,
Wi' gentles thou erects thy head ;
Yet humbly kind, in time o' need,
        The poor man's wine,
His wee drap parritch, or his bread,
        Thou kitchens fine.

Thou art the life o' public haunts ;
But thee, what were our fairs and rants ?
Ev'n godly meetings o' the saunts,
        By thee inspir'd,
When gaping they besiege the tents,
        Are doubly fir'd.

That merry night we get the corn in !
O sweetly then thou reams the horn in !
Or reekin' on a New-Year mornin'
                    In cog or bicker,
An' just a wee drap sp'ritual burn in,
                    An' gusty sucker !

When Vulcan gies his bellows breath,
An' ploughmen gather wi' their graith,
O rare to see thee fizz an' freath
                    I' th' luggèd caup !
Then Burnewin comes on like death
                    At ev'ry chaup.

Nae mercy, then, for airn or steel ;
The brawnie, banie, ploughman chiel,
Brings hard owrehip, wi' sturdy wheel,
                    The strong forehammer,
Till block an' studdie ring an' reel
                    Wi' dinsome clamour.

When skirlin' weanies see the light,
Thou maks the gossips clatter bright
How fumblin' cuifs their dearies slight—
                    Wae worth the name !
Nae howdie gets a social night,
                    Or plack frae them.

When neibors anger at a plea,
An' just as wud as wud can be,
How easy can the barley-bree
                    Cement the quarrel !
It 's aye the cheapest lawyer's fee
                    To taste the barrel.

Alake ! that e'er my Muse has reason
To wyte her countrymen wi' treason ;
But mony daily weet their weasan'
                    Wi' liquors nice,
An' hardly, in a winter's season,
                    E'er spier her price.

Wae worth that brandy, burning trash !
Fell source o' mony a pain an' brash !
Twins mony a poor, doylt, drucken hash,
                    O' half his days ;
An' sends, beside, auld Scotland's cash
                    To her warst faes.

Ye Scots, wha wish auld Scotland well,
Ye chief, to you my tale I tell,
Poor plackless devils like mysel' !
                    It sets you ill,
Wi' bitter, dearthfu' wines to mell,
                    Or foreign gill.

May gravels round his blather wrench,
An' gouts torment him, inch by inch,
Wha twists his gruntle wi' a glunch
        O' sour disdain,
Out owre a glass o' whisky punch
        Wɪ' honest men ! . . .

Thee, Ferintosh ! O sadly lost !
Scotland, lament frae coast to coast !
Now colic-grips an' barkin' hoast
        May kill us a' ;
For loyal Forbes' charter'd boast
        Is ta'en awa !

Thae curst horse-leeches o' th' Excise,
Wha mak the whisky stells their prize—
Haud up thy hand, deil !   Ance—twice—thrice !
        There, seize the blinkers !
An' bake them up in brunstane pies
        For poor damn'd drinkers.

Fortune ! if thou'll but gie me still
Hale breeks, a bannock, and a gill,
An' rowth o' rhyme to rave at will,
        Tak' a' the rest,
An' deal'd about as thy blind skill
        Directs thee best.

OF A' THE AIRTS

Of a' the airts the wind can blaw,
   I dearly like the west,
For there the bonnie lassie lives,
   The lassie I lo'e best :
There 's wild woods grow, and rivers row,
   And mony a hill between ;
But day and night my fancy's flight
   Is ever wi' my Jean.

I see her in the dewy flowers,
   I see her sweet and fair :
I hear her in the tunefu' birds,
   I hear her charm the air :
There 's not a bonnie flower that springs
   By fountain, shaw, or green ;
There 's not a bonnie bird that sings,
   But minds me o' my Jean.

IT IS NA, JEAN, THY BONNIE FACE

It is na, Jean, thy bonnie face,
    Nor shape that I admire,
Although thy beauty and thy grace
    Might weel awake desire.

Something, in ilka part o' thee,
    To praise, to love, I find ;
But dear as is thy form to me,
    Still dearer is thy mind.

Nae mair ungenerous wish I hae,
    Nor stronger in my breast,
Than if I canna mak thee sae,
    At least to see thee blest.

Content am I, if Heaven shall give
    But happiness to thee :
And as wi' thee I 'd wish to live,
    For thee I 'd bear to die.

UP IN THE MORNING

Up in the morning 's no' for me,
   Up in the morning early ;
When a' the hills are covered wi' snaw,
   I 'm sure it 's winter fairly.

Cauld blaws the wind frae east to wast,
   The drift is driving sairly ;
Sae loud and shrill 's I hear the blast,
   I 'm sure it 's winter fairly.

The birds sit chittering in the thorn,
   A' day they fare but sparely ;
And lang 's the night frae e'en to morn,
   I 'm sure it 's winter fairly.

O WERE I ON PARNASSUS HILL

O were I on Parnassus hill,
Or had o' Helicon my fill,
That I might catch poetic skill,
    To sing how dear I love thee !
But Nith maun be my Muse's well,
My Muse maun be thy bonnie sel',
On Corsincon I 'll glow'r and spell,
    And write how dear I love thee.

Then come, sweet Muse, inspire my lay !
For a' the lee-lang simmer's day
I couldna sing, I couldna say,
    How much, how dear, I love thee.
I see thee dancing o'er the green,
Thy waist sae jimp, thy limbs sae clean,
Thy tempting lips, thy roguish e'en—
    By Heaven and Earth I love thee !

By night, by day, a-field, at hame,
The thoughts o' thee my breast inflame :
And aye I muse and sing thy name—
    I only live to love thee.
Tho' I were doom'd to wander on,
Beyond the sea, beyond the sun,
Till my last weary sand was run,
    Till then—and then—I 'd love thee !

MY WIFE'S A WINSOME WEE THING

She is a winsome wee thing,
She is a handsome wee thing,
She is a bonnie wee thing,
    This sweet wee wife o' mine.

I never saw a fairer,
I never lo'ed a dearer,
And neist my heart I'll wear her,
    For fear my jewel tine.

She is a winsome wee thing,
She is a handsome wee thing,
She is a bonnie wee thing,
    This sweet wee wife o' mine.

The warld's wrack, we share o't,
The warstle and the care o't;
Wi' her I'll blythely bear it,
    And think my lot divine.

THE DEATH AND DYING WORDS OF POOR MAILIE, THE AUTHOR'S ONLY PET YOWE

As Mailie, an' her lambs thegither,
Was ae day nibbling on the tether,
Upon her cloot she coost a hitch,
An' owre she warsled in the ditch ;
There, groaning, dying, she did lie,
When Hughoc he cam doytin by.
    Wi' glowrin' een, an' lifted han's,
Poor Hughoc like a statue stan's ;
He saw her days were near-hand ended,
But, wae 's my heart ! he could na mend it !
He gapèd wide, but naething spak ;
At length poor Mailie silence brak :—

'O thou, whase lamentable face
Appears to mourn my woefu' case !
My dying words attentive hear,
An' bear them to my Master dear.
    'Tell him, if e'er again he keep
As muckle gear as buy a sheep,—
O bid him never tie them mair
Wi' wicked strings o' hemp or hair !
But ca' them out to park or hill,
An' let them wander at their will ;
So may his flock increase, an' grow
To scores o' lambs, an' packs o' woo' !
    'Tell him he was a Master kin',

An' aye was guid to me an' mine ;
An' now my dying charge I gie him,
My helpless lambs, I trust them wi' him.
　'O bid him save their harmless lives
Frae dogs, an' tods, an' butchers' knives !
But gie them guid cow-milk their fill,
Till they be fit to fend themsel :
An' tent them duly, e'en an' morn,
Wi' teats o' hay an' ripps o' corn.
　'An' may they never learn the gates
Of ither vile wanrestfu' pets—
To slink thro' slaps, an' reave an' steal,
At stacks o' pease, or stocks o' kail.
So may they, like their great forbears,
For mony a year come thro' the shears ;
So wives will gie them bits o' bread,
An' bairns greet for them when they're dead.
　'My poor tup-lamb, my son an' heir,
O bid him breed him up wi' care !
An', if he live to be a beast,
To pit some havins in his breast !

An' warn him, what I winna name,
To stay content wi' yowes at hame ;
An' no to rin an' wear his cloots,
Like ither menseless graceless brutes.
  ' An' neist my yowie, silly thing,
Gude keep thee frae a tether string !
O may thou ne'er forgather up
Wi' ony blastit moorland tup ;
But ay keep mind to moop an' mell,
Wi' sheep o' credit like thysel !
  ' And now, my bairns, wi' my last breath
I lea'e my blessin wi' you baith ;
An' when you think upo' your mither,
Mind to be kind to ane anither.
  ' Now, honest Hughoc, dinna fail
To tell my master a' my tale ;
An' bid him burn this cursed tether ;
An', for thy pains, thou 'se get my blether.'

  This said, poor Mailie turn'd her head,
An' closed her een amang the dead !

POOR MAILIE'S ELEGY

Lament in rhyme, lament in prose,
Wi' saut tears tricklin' down your nose;
Our bardie's fate is at a close,
              Past a' remead;
The last sad cape-stane of his woes—
              Poor Mailie's dead!

It's no the loss o' warl's gear
That could sae bitter draw the tear,
Or mak our bardie, dowie, wear
              The mourning weed:
He's lost a friend and neibor dear
              In Mailie dead.

Thro' a' the toun she trotted by him;
A lang half-mile she could descry him;
Wi' kindly bleat, when she did spy him,
              She ran wi' speed:
A friend mair faithfu' ne'er cam nigh him
              Than Mailie dead.

I wat she was a sheep o' sense,
An' could behave hersel wi' mense;
I'll say 't, she never brak a fence
              Thro' thievish greed.
Our bardie, lanely, keeps the spence
              Sin' Mailie's dead.

Or, if he wanders up the howe,
Her living image in her yowe
Comes bleating to him, owre the knowe,
            For bits o' bread,
An' down the briny pearls rowe
            For Mailie dead.

She was nae get o' moorland tups,
Wi' tawted ket, an' hairy hips ;
For her forbears were brought in ships
            Frae yont the Tweed :
A bonnier fleesh ne'er cross'd the clips
            Than Mailie's, dead.

Wae worth the man wha first did shape
That vile wanchancie thing—a rape !
It maks guid fellows girn an' gape,
            Wi' chokin' dread ;
An' Robin's bonnet wave wi' crape
            For Mailie dead.

O a' ye bards on bonnie Doon !
An' wha on Ayr your chanters tune !
Come, join the melancholious croon
            O' Robin's reed ;
His heart will never get aboon
            His Mailie dead !

THE BONNIE LAD THAT'S FAR AWA

O how can I be blithe and glad,
   Or how can I gang brisk and braw,
When the bonnie lad that I lo'e best
   Is o'er the hills and far awa?

It's no the frosty winter wind,
   It's no the driving drift and snaw;
But aye the tear comes in my e'e,
   To think on him that's far awa.

My father pat me frae his door,
   My friends they hae disown'd me a':
But I hae ane will tak my part,
   The bonnie lad that's far awa.

A pair o' gloves he bought to me,
   And silken snoods he gae me twa;
And I will wear them for his sake,
   The bonnie lad that's far awa.

O weary winter soon will pass,
   And spring will cleed the birken shaw:
And my young babie will be born,
   And he'll be hame that's far awa.

ADDRESS TO THE UNCO GUID, OR THE RIGIDLY RIGHTEOUS

My son, these maxims make a rule,
And lump them aye thegither :
The rigid righteous is a fool,
The rigid wise anither :
The cleanest corn that e'er was dight,
May hae some pyles o' caff in ;
So ne'er a fellow-creature slight
For random fits o' daffin.

SOLOMON (Eccles. vii. 16).

O ye wha are sae guid yoursel,
    Sae pious and sae holy,
Ye've nought to do but mark and tell
    Your neibour's fauts and folly !
Whase life is like a weel-gaun mill,
    Supplied wi' store o' water :
The heapèd happer's ebbing still,
    And still the clap plays clatter :

Hear me, ye venerable core,
    As counsel for poor mortals,
That frequent pass douce Wisdom's door,
    For glaikit Folly's portals ;
I, for their thoughtless careless sakes,
    Would here propone defences,—
Their donsie tricks, their black mistakes,
    Their failings and mischances.

Ye see your state wi' theirs compar'd,
    And shudder at the niffer ;
But cast a moment's fair regard—
    What maks the mighty differ ?
Discount what scant occasion gave
    That purity ye pride in,
And (what's aft mair than a' the lave)
    Your better art o' hidin'.

Think, when your castigated pulse
    Gies now and then a wallop,
What ragings must his veins convulse,
    That still eternal gallop !
Wi' wind and tide fair i' your tail,
    Right on ye scud your sea-way ;
But in the teeth o' baith to sail,
    It maks an unco leeway.

See Social life and Glee sit down,
    All joyous and unthinking,
Till, quite transmogrified, they're grown
    Debauchery and Drinking :
O would they stay to calculate
    Th' eternal consequences ;
Or your more dreaded hell to state,
    Damnation of expenses !

Ye high, exalted, virtuous Dames,
    Tied up in godly laces,
Before ye gie poor Frailty names,
    Suppose a change o' cases ;
A dear lov'd lad, convenience snug,
    A treacherous inclination—
But, let me whisper i' your lug,
    Ye're aiblins nae temptation.

Then gently scan your brother man,
    Still gentler sister woman ;
Tho' they may gang a kennin wrang,
    To step aside is human.
One point must still be greatly dark,
    The moving why they do it ;
And just as lamely can ye mark
    How far perhaps they rue it.

Who made the heart, 'tis He alone
    Decidedly can try us ;
He knows each chord, its various tone,
    Each spring, its various bias.
Then at the balance let's be mute,
    We never can adjust it ;
What's done we partly may compute,
    But know not what's resisted.

CA' THE YOWES TO THE KNOWES

Hark ! the mavis' e'ening sang,
Sounding Clouden's woods amang ;
Then a-faulding let us gang,
  My bonnie dearie.

   Ca' the yowes to the knowes,
   Ca' them where the heather grows,
   Ca' them where the burnie rowes,
     My bonnie dearie.

We'll gae down by Clouden side,
Thro' the hazels, spreading wide,
O'er the waves that sweetly glide,
  To the moon sae clearly.

Yonder 's Clouden's silent towers,
Where at moonshine midnight hours,
O'er the dewy bending flowers,
  Fairies dance sae cheery.

Ghaist nor bogle shalt thou fear ;
Thou 'rt to love and Heav'n sae dear,
Nocht of ill may come thee near,
  My bonnie dearie.

Fair and lovely as thou art,
Thou hast stown my very heart ;
I can die--but canna part,
  My bonnie dearie.

   Ca' the yowes to the knowes,
   Ca' them where the heather grows,
   Ca' them where the burnie rowes,
     My bonnie dearie.

YE BANKS AND BRAES

YE banks and braes o' bonnie Doon,
    How can ye bloom sae fresh and fair ?
How can ye chant, ye little birds,
    And I sae weary fu' o' care ?

Thou 'lt break my heart, thou warbling bird,
    That wantons thro' the flowering thorn :
Thou minds me o' departed joys,
    Departed never to return.

Aft hae I rov'd by bonnie Doon,
    To see the rose and woodbine twine ;
And ilka bird sang o' its love,
    And fondly sae did I o' mine.

Wi' lightsome heart I pu'd a rose,
    Fu' sweet upon its thorny tree ;
And my fause lover stole my rose,
    But ah ! he left the thorn wi' me.

NOW WESTLIN WINDS

Now westlin winds and slaughtering guns
    Bring autumn's pleasant weather ;
The moorcock springs, on whirring wings,
    Amang the blooming heather :
Now waving grain, wide o'er the plain,
    Delights the weary farmer ;
And the moon shines bright, when I rove at night
    To muse upon my charmer.

The partridge loves the fruitful fells ;
    The plover loves the mountains ;

The woodcock haunts the lonely dells ;
    The soaring hern the fountains :
Thro' lofty groves the cushat roves,
    The path of man to shun it ;
The hazel bush o'erhangs the thrush,
    The spreading thorn the linnet.

Thus ev'ry kind their pleasure find,
    The savage and the tender ;
Some social join, and leagues combine ;
    Some solitary wander ;
Avaunt, away ! the cruel sway,
    Tyrannic man's dominion ;
The sportsman's joy, the murdering cry,
    The fluttering, gory pinion !

But, Peggy dear, the ev'ning's clear,
  Thick flies the skimming swallow;
The sky is blue, the fields in view,
  All fading-green and yellow:
Come let us stray our gladsome way,
  And view the charms of nature;
The rustling corn, the fruited thorn,
  And every happy creature.

We'll gently walk, and sweetly talk,
  Till the silent moon shine clearly;
I'll grasp thy waist, and, fondly prest,
  Swear how I love thee dearly:
Not vernal show'rs to budding flow'rs,
  Not autumn to the farmer,
So dear can be as thou to me,
  My fair, my lovely charmer!

MY HEART'S IN THE HIGHLANDS

My heart's in the Highlands, my heart is not here ;
My heart's in the Highlands a-chasing the deer ;
Chasing the wild deer, and following the roe,
My heart's in the Highlands, wherever I go !

Farewell to the Highlands, farewell to the North,
The birth-place of valour, the country of worth !
Wherever I wander, wherever I rove,
The hills of the Highlands for ever I love.

Farewell to the mountains, high cover'd with snow ;
Farewell to the straths and green valleys below ;
Farewell to the forests and wild-hanging woods ;
Farewell to the torrents and loud-pouring floods !

My heart's in the Highlands, my heart is not here ;
My heart's in the Highlands a-chasing the deer ;
Chasing the wild deer, and following the roe,
My heart's in the Highlands, wherever I go !

'BRAW SOBER LESSONS'

(EPISTLE TO A YOUNG FRIEND)

I LANG hae thought, my youthfu' friend,
    A something to have sent you,
Tho' it should serve nae ither end
    Than just a kind memento ;
But how the subject theme may gang,
    Let time and chance determine ;
Perhaps it may turn out a sang,
    Perhaps turn out a sermon.

Ye 'll try the world soon, my lad,
    And, Andrew dear, believe me,
Ye 'll find mankind an unco squad,
    And muckle they may grieve ye :
For care and trouble set your thought,
    Ev'n when your end 's attained ;
And a' your views may come to nought,
    Where ev'ry nerve is strained.

I 'll no say men are villains a' ;
    The real harden'd wicked,
Wha hae nae check but human law,
    Are to a few restricked :
But oh ! mankind are unco weak,
    An' little to be trusted ;
If self the wavering balance shake,
    It 's rarely right adjusted !

Yet they wha fa' in fortune's strife,
    Their fate we shouldna censure ;
For still th' important end of life
    They equally may answer.
A man may hae an honest heart,
    Tho' poortith hourly stare him ;
A man may tak a neibor's part,
    Yet hae nae cash to spare him.

Aye free, aff han', your story tell,
    When wi' a bosom crony ;
But still keep something to yoursel
    Ye scarcely tell to ony.
Conceal yoursel as weel's ye can
    Frae critical dissection ;
But keek thro' ev'ry other man
    Wi' sharpen'd sly inspection.

The sacred lowe o' weel-plac'd love,
    Luxuriantly indulge it ;
But never tempt th' illicit rove,
    Tho' naething should divulge it :
I wave the quantum o' the sin,
    The hazard of concealing ;
But oh ! it hardens a' within,
    And petrifies the feeling !

To catch dame Fortune's golden smile,
    Assiduous wait upon her ;
And gather gear by ev'ry wile
    That's justified by honour ;
Not for to hide it in a hedge,
    Nor for a train attendant ;
But for the glorious privilege
    Of being independent.

The fear o' hell's a hangman's whip
    To haud the wretch in order ;
But where ye feel your honour grip,
    Let that aye be your border :
Its slightest touches, instant pause—
    Debar a' side pretences ;
And resolutely keep its laws,
    Uncaring consequences.

The great Creator to revere
    Must sure become the creature ;
But still the preaching cant forbear,
    And ev'n the rigid feature :
Yet ne'er with wits profane to range
    Be complaisance extended ;
An atheist laugh 's a poor exchange
    For Deity offended.

When ranting round in pleasure's ring,
    Religion may be blinded ;
Or, if she gie a random sting,
    It may be little minded ;
But when on life we're tempest-driv'n,
    A conscience but a canker—
A correspondence fix'd wi' Heav'n
    Is sure a noble anchor.

Adieu, dear amiable youth !
    Your heart can ne'er be wanting !
May prudence, fortitude, and truth
    Erect your brow undaunting.
In ploughman phrase, God send you speed
    Still daily to grow wiser ;
And may ye better reck the rede
    Than ever did th' adviser !

COMING THROUGH THE RYE

Jenny's a' wat, poor body ;
Jenny's seldom dry ;
She draiglet a' her petticoatie,
Coming through the rye.

Coming through the rye, poor body,
Coming through the rye,
She draiglet a' her petticoatie,
Coming through the rye.

Gin a body meet a body
Coming through the rye ;
Gin a body kiss a body,
Need a body cry ?

Gin a body meet a body
Coming through the glen ;
Gin a body kiss a body,
Need the world ken ?

TO A HAGGIS

Fair fa' your honest sonsie face,
Great chieftain o' the puddin'-race !
Aboon them a' ye tak your place,
      Painch, tripe, or thairm :
Weel are ye wordy o' a grace
      As lang 's my arm.

The groaning trencher there ye fill,
Your hurdies like a distant hill ;
Your pin wad help to mend a mill
      In time o' need ;
While thro' your pores the dews distil
      Like amber bead.

His knife see rustic Labour dight,
An' cut you up wi' ready sleight,
Trenching your gushing entrails bright
      Like ony ditch ;
And then, O what a glorious sight,
      Warm-reekin', rich !

Then, horn for horn they stretch an' strive,
Deil tak the hindmost ! on they drive,
Till a' their weel-swall'd kytes belyve
      Are bent like drums ;
Then auld guidman, maist like to rive,
      Bethankit hums.

Is there that o'er his French ragout,
Or olio that wad staw a sow,
Or fricassee wad mak her spew
            Wi' perfect sconner,
Looks down wi' sneering scornfu' view
            On sic a dinner?

Poor devil! see him owre his trash,
As feckless as a wither'd rash,
His spindle shank a guid whip-lash,
            His nieve a nit:
Thro' bloody flood or field to dash,
            O how unfit!

But mark the Rustic, haggis-fed—
The trembling earth resounds his tread!
Clap in his walie nieve a blade,
            He'll mak it whissle;
An' legs, an' arms, an' heads will sned,
            Like taps o' thrissle.

Ye Pow'rs, wha mak mankind your care,
And dish them out their bill o' fare,
Auld Scotland wants nae skinking ware
            That jaups in luggies;
But, if ye wish her gratefu' prayer,
            Gie her a Haggis!

LAMENT FOR JAMES,
EARL OF GLENCAIRN

THE wind blew hollow frae the hills ;
    By fits the sun's departing beam
Look'd on the fading yellow woods
    That waved o'er Lugar's winding stream.
Beneath a craigy steep, a bard,
    Laden with years and meikle pain,
In loud lament bewail'd his lord,
    Whom death had all untimely taen.

He lean'd him to an ancient aik,
    Whose trunk was mould'ring down with years ;
His locks were bleachèd white wi' time,
    His hoary cheek was wet wi' tears ;
And as he touch'd his trembling harp,
    And as he tun'd his doleful sang,
The winds, lamenting thro' their caves,
    To echo bore the notes alang.

' Ye scatter'd birds that faintly sing,
    The reliques of the vernal quire !
Ye woods that shed on a' the winds
    The honours of the agèd year !
A few short months, and glad and gay,
    Again ye 'll charm the ear and e'e ;
But nocht in all revolving time
    Can gladness bring again to me.

'I am a bending agèd tree,
    That long has stood the wind and rain ;
But now has come a cruel blast,
    And my last hold of earth is gane :
Nae leaf o' mine shall greet the spring,
    Nae simmer sun exalt my bloom ;
But I maun lie before the storm,
    And others plant them in my room.

'I've seen so many changefu' years,
    On earth I am a stranger grown ;
I wander in the ways of men,
    Alike unknowing and unknown :
Unheard, unpitied, unreliev'd,
    I bear alane my lade o' care,
For silent, low, on beds of dust,
    Lie a' that would my sorrows share.

'And last (the sum of a' my griefs !)
    My noble master lies in clay ;
The flow'r amang our barons bold,
    His country's pride, his country's stay :
In weary being now I pine
    For a' the life of life is dead,
And hope has left my agèd ken,
    On forward wing for ever fled.

'Awake thy last sad voice, my harp!
    The voice of woe and wild despair;
Awake, resound thy latest lay,
    Then sleep in silence evermair!
And thou, my last, best, only friend,
    That fillest an untimely tomb,
Accept this tribute from the bard
    Thou brought from fortune's mirkest gloom.

'In poverty's low barren vale,
    Thick mists obscure involv'd me round;
Though oft I turn'd the wistful eye,
    No ray of fame was to be found:
Thou found'st me, like the morning sun
    That melts the fogs in limpid air;
The friendless bard and rustic song
    Became alike thy fostering care.

'O why has worth so short a date
    While villains ripen grey with time?
Must thou, the noble, gen'rous, great,
    Fall in bold manhood's hardy prime?
Why did I live to see that day,
    A day to me so full of woe?
O had I met the mortal shaft
    Which laid my benefactor low!

'The bridegroom may forget the bride
    Was made his wedded wife yestreen;
The monarch may forget the crown
    That on his head an hour has been;
The mother may forget the child
    That smiles sae sweetly on her knee;
But I'll remember thee, Glencairn,
    And a' that thou hast done for me!'

A PRAYER IN THE PROSPECT OF DEATH

O THOU unknown Almighty Cause
    Of all my hope and fear !
In whose dread presence, ere an hour,
    Perhaps I must appear !

If I have wander'd in those paths
    Of life I ought to shun ;
As something, loudly in my breast,
    Remonstrates I have done ;

Thou know'st that Thou hast formèd me
    With passions wild and strong ;
And list'ning to their witching voice
    Has often led me wrong.

Where human weakness has come short,
    Or frailty stept aside,
Do thou, All-Good ! for such Thou art,
    In shades of darkness hide.

Where with intention I have err'd,
    No other plea I have,
But Thou art good ; and Goodness still
    Delighteth to forgive.

STANZAS ON THE SAME OCCASION

Why am I loath to leave this earthly scene ?
　　Have I so found it full of pleasing charms ?
Some drops of joy with draughts of ill between ;
　　Some gleams of sunshine 'mid renewing storms !
Is it departing pangs my soul alarms ?
　　Or Death's unlovely, dreary, dark abode ?
For guilt, for guilt, my terrors are in arms ;
　　I tremble to approach an angry God,
And justly smart beneath his sin-avenging rod.

Fain would I say, ' Forgive my foul offence ! '
　　Fain promise never more to disobey ;
But, should my Author health again dispense,
　　Again I might desert fair virtue's way ;
Again in folly's path might go astray ;
　　Again exalt the brute, and sink the man ;
Then how should I for Heavenly mercy pray,
　　Who act so counter Heavenly mercy's plan ?
Who sin so oft have mourn'd, yet to temptation ran ?

O Thou, great Governor of all below !
　　If I may dare a lifted eye to Thee,
Thy nod can make the tempest cease to blow,
　　And still the tumult of the raging sea :
With that controlling pow'r assist ev'n me
　　Those headlong furious passions to confine,
For all unfit I feel my powers to be,
　　To rule their torrent in th' allowèd line ;
O, aid me with Thy help, Omnipotence Divine !

A BARD'S EPITAPH

Is there a whim-inspirèd fool,
Owre fast for thought, owre hot for rule,
Owre blate to seek, owre proud to snool,
      Let him draw near ;
And owre this grassy heap sing dool,
      And drap a tear.

Is there a bard of rustic song,
Who, noteless, steals the crowds among,
That weekly this area throng,
      O, pass not by !
But, with a frater-feeling strong,
      Here heave a sigh.

Is there a man whose judgment clear,
Can others teach the course to steer,
Yet runs, himself, life's mad career,
      Wild as the wave ;
Here pause—and, thro' the starting tear,
      Survey this grave.

The poor inhabitant below
Was quick to learn and wise to know,
And keenly felt the friendly glow,
      And softer flame ;
But thoughtless follies laid him low,
      And stain'd his name !

Reader, attend ! whether thy soul
Soars fancy's flights beyond the pole,
Or darkling grubs this earthly hole,
      In low pursuit ;
Know prudent cautious self-control
      Is wisdom's root.

THE BRAES O' BALLOCHMYLE

The Catrine woods were yellow seen,
    The flowers decayed on Catrine lee,
Nae lav'rock sang on hillock green,
    But nature sickened on the e'e.
Thro' faded groves Maria sang,
    Hersel in beauty's bloom the whyle,
And aye the wild-wood echoes rang,
    ' Fareweel the braes o' Ballochmyle !

' Low in your wintry beds, ye flowers,
    Again ye 'll flourish fresh and fair ;
Ye birdies dumb, in withering bowers,
    Again ye 'll charm the vocal air.
But here, alas ! for me nae mair
    Shall birdie charm, or floweret smile ;
Fareweel, the bonnie banks of Ayr,
    Fareweel, fareweel, sweet Ballochmyle !'

IN EVIL DAYS

(FROM A LETTER TO GRAHAM OF FINTRY, 1791)

I DREAD thee, Fate, relentless and severe,
With all a poet's, husband's, father's fear !
Already one strong-hold of hope is lost,
Glencairn, the truly noble, lies in dust—
Fled, like the sun eclips'd as noon appears,
And left us darkling in a world of tears.
Oh ! hear my ardent, grateful, selfish pray'r !
Fintry, my other stay, long bless and spare !
Thro' a long life his hopes and wishes crown,
And bright in cloudless skies his sun go down !

SCOTS WHA HAE

ROBERT BRUCE'S ADDRESS TO HIS ARMY, BEFORE
THE BATTLE OF BANNOCKBURN

Scots, wha hae wi' Wallace bled,
Scots, wham Bruce has aften led,
Welcome to your gory bed,
    Or to victorie.

Now's the day, and now's the hour ;
See the front o' battle lour !
See approach proud Edward's power—
    Chains and slaverie !

Wha will be a traitor knave ?
Wha can fill a coward's grave ?
Wha sae base as be a slave ?
    Let him turn and flee !

Wha for Scotland's King and law
Freedom's sword will strongly draw,
Freeman stand, or freeman fa' ?
    Let him follow me !

By oppression's woes and pains !
By your sons in servile chains !
We will drain our dearest veins,
    But they shall be free !

Lay the proud usurpers low !
Tyrants fall in every foe !
Liberty's in every blow !
    Let us do or die !

DOES HAUGHTY GAUL

Does haughty Gaul invasion threat ?
  Then let the loons beware, Sir,
There's wooden walls upon our seas,
  And volunteers on shore, Sir.
The Nith shall run to Corsincon,
  And Criffel sink in Solway,
Ere we permit a foreign foe
  On British ground to rally !

O let us not like snarling tykes
  In wrangling be divided,
Till, slap ! come in an unco loon
  And wi' a rung decide it.
Be Britain still to Britain true,
  Amang oursels united ;
For never but by British hands
  Maun British wrangs be righted !

The kettle o' the kirk and state,
  Perhaps a clout may fail in 't ;
But deil a foreign tinkler loon
  Shall ever ca' a nail in 't.

Our father 's blude the kettle bought,
  An' wha wad dare to spoil it?
By heavens ! the sacrilegious dog
  Shall fuel be to boil it !

The wretch that would a tyrant own,
  And the wretch, his true-sworn brother,
Who'd set the mob aboon the throne,—
  May they be damned together !
Who will not sing *God save the King !*
  Shall hang as high 's the steeple ;
But while we sing *God save the King !*
  We 'll not forget the people !

THE COTTER'S SATURDAY NIGHT

NOVEMBER chill blaws loud wi' angry sough ;
    The short'ning winter-day is near a close ;
The miry beasts retreating frae the pleugh ;
    The black'ning trains o' craws to their repose :
    The toil-worn Cotter frae his labour goes,
This night his weekly moil is at an end,
    Collects his spades, his mattocks, and his hoes,
Hoping the morn in ease and rest to spend,
And weary, o'er the moor, his course does
        hameward bend.

At length his lonely cot appears in view,
    Beneath the shelter of an agèd tree ;
Th' expectant wee-things, toddlin', stacher through
    To meet their Dad, wi' flichterin' noise an' glee.
    His wee bit ingle, blinkin bonnilie,
His clean hearth-stane, his thrifty wifie 's smile,
    The lisping infant prattling on his knee,
Does a' his weary kiaugh and care beguile,
An' makes him quite forget his labour an' his toil.

Belyve, the elder bairns come drapping in,
    At service out, amang the farmers roun' ;
Some ca' the pleugh, some herd, some tentie rin
    A cannie errand to a neibor town :
    Their eldest hope, their Jenny, woman-grown,
In youthfu' bloom, love sparkling in her e'e,
    Comes hame, perhaps to shew a braw new gown,
Or deposite her sair-won penny-fee,
To help her parents dear, if they in hardship be.

With joy unfeign'd brothers and sisters meet,
　　An' each for other's weelfare kindly spiers :
The social hours, swift-wing'd, unnoticed fleet ;
　　Each tells the uncos that he sees or hears ;
　　The parents, partial, eye their hopeful years ;
Anticipation forward points the view.
　　The mother, wi' her needle an' her sheers,
Gars auld claes look amaist as weel 's the new ;
The father mixes a' wi' admonition due.

Their master's an' their mistress's command,
　　The younkers a' are warnèd to obey ;
An' mind their labours wi' an eydent hand,
　　An' ne'er, tho' out o' sight, to jauk or play :
　　'And O ! be sure to fear the Lord alway,
An' mind your duty, duly, morn an' night !
　　Lest in temptation's path ye gang astray,
Implore His counsel and assisting might :
They never sought in vain that sought the Lord aright !'

But hark ! a rap comes gently to the door ;
　　Jenny, wha kens the meaning o' the same,
Tells how a neibor lad cam o'er the moor,
　　To do some errands, and convoy her hame.
　　The wily mother sees the conscious flame
Sparkle in Jenny's e'e, and flush her cheek ;
　　Wi' heart-struck anxious care, inquires his name,
While Jenny hafflins is afraid to speak ;
Weel pleased the mother hears it 's nae wild worthless rake.

Wi' kindly welcome, Jenny brings him ben ;
　　A strappin' youth ; he takes the mother's eye ;
Blythe Jenny sees the visit 's no ill ta'en ;
　　The father cracks of horses, pleughs, and kye.

The youngster's artless heart o'erflows wi' joy,
But blate and laithfu', scarce can weel behave ;
The mother, wi' a woman's wiles, can spy
What makes the youth sae bashfu' an' sae grave ;
Weel-pleased to think her bairn 's respected like the lave.

O happy love ! where love like this is found ;
O heart-felt raptures ! bliss beyond compare !
I've pacèd much this weary mortal round,
And sage experience bids me this declare—
' If Heaven a draught of heavenly pleasure spare,
One cordial in this melancholy vale,
'Tis when a youthful, loving, modest pair
In other's arms breathe out the tender tale,
Beneath the milk-white thorn that scents the evening gale.'

Is there, in human form, that bears a heart—
A wretch, a villain, lost to love and truth—
That can, with studied, sly, ensnaring art,
Betray sweet Jenny's unsuspecting youth ?
Curse on his perjur'd arts, dissembling smooth !
Are honour, virtue, conscience, all exil'd ?
Is there no pity, no relenting ruth,
Points to the parents fondling o'er their child ?
Then paints the ruin'd maid, and their distraction wild ?

But now the supper crowns their simple board,
The halesome parritch, chief of Scotia's food :
The sowpe their only hawkie does afford,
That 'yont the hallan snugly chows her cood ;
The dame brings forth in complimental mood,
To grace the lad, her weel-hain'd kebbuck, fell ;
And aft he 's prest, and aft he ca's it good ;
The frugal wifie, garrulous, will tell
How 'twas a towmond auld sin' lint was i' the bell.

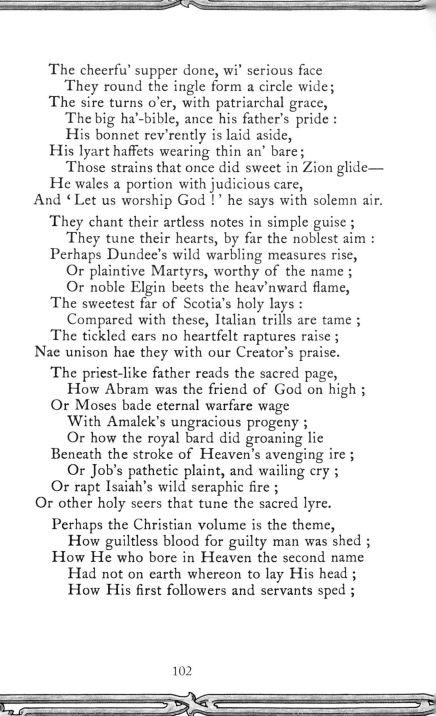

The cheerfu' supper done, wi' serious face
    They round the ingle form a circle wide;
The sire turns o'er, with patriarchal grace,
    The big ha'-bible, ance his father's pride :
    His bonnet rev'rently is laid aside,
His lyart haffets wearing thin an' bare;
    Those strains that once did sweet in Zion glide—
He wales a portion with judicious care,
And 'Let us worship God !' he says with solemn air.

They chant their artless notes in simple guise ;
    They tune their hearts, by far the noblest aim :
Perhaps Dundee's wild warbling measures rise,
    Or plaintive Martyrs, worthy of the name ;
    Or noble Elgin beets the heav'nward flame,
The sweetest far of Scotia's holy lays :
    Compared with these, Italian trills are tame ;
The tickled ears no heartfelt raptures raise ;
Nae unison hae they with our Creator's praise.

The priest-like father reads the sacred page,
    How Abram was the friend of God on high ;
Or Moses bade eternal warfare wage
    With Amalek's ungracious progeny ;
    Or how the royal bard did groaning lie
Beneath the stroke of Heaven's avenging ire ;
    Or Job's pathetic plaint, and wailing cry ;
Or rapt Isaiah's wild seraphic fire ;
Or other holy seers that tune the sacred lyre.

Perhaps the Christian volume is the theme,
    How guiltless blood for guilty man was shed ;
How He who bore in Heaven the second name
    Had not on earth whereon to lay His head ;
    How His first followers and servants sped ;

The precepts sage they wrote to many a land :
   How he, was lone in Patmos banishèd,
Saw in the sun a mighty angel stand,
And heard great Bab'lon's doom pronounced by Heaven's
   command.

Then kneeling down to Heaven's Eternal King
   The saint, the father, and the husband prays :
Hope ' springs exulting on triumphant wing '
   That thus they all shall meet in future days :
   There ever bask in uncreated rays,
No more to sigh, or shed the bitter tear,
   Together hymning their Creator's praise,
In such society, yet still more dear ;
While circling Time moves round in an eternal sphere.

Compared with this, how poor Religion's pride,
   In all the pomp of method and of art,
When men display to congregations wide
   Devotion's every grace, except the heart !
   The Power, incensed, the pageant will desert,
The pompous strain, the sacerdotal stole ;
   But haply, in some cottage far apart,
May hear, well pleased, the language of the soul ;
And in His Book of Life the inmates poor enrol.

Then homeward all take off their several way ;
   The youngling cottagers retire to rest :
The parent-pair their secret homage pay,
   And proffer up to Heav'n the warm request,
   That He who stills the raven's clamorous nest,
And decks the lily fair in flowery pride,
   Would, in the way His wisdom sees the best,
For them and for their little ones provide ;
But chiefly in their hearts with grace divine preside.

From scenes like these old Scotia's grandeur springs,
    That makes her loved at home, revered abroad :
Princes and lords are but the breath of kings,
    'An honest man 's the noblest work of God ' ;
    And certes, in fair virtue's heavenly road,
The cottage leaves the palace far behind ;
    What is a lordling's pomp ? a cumbrous load,
Disguising oft the wretch of human kind,
Studied in arts of hell, in wickedness refin'd !

O Scotia ! my dear, my native soil ;
    For whom my warmest wish to Heaven is sent !
Long may thy hardy sons of rustic toil
    Be blest with health, and peace, and sweet content !
    And O may Heaven their simple lives prevent
From luxury's contagion, weak and vile ;
    Then, howe'er crowns and coronets be rent,
A virtuous populace may rise the while,
And stand a wall of fire around their much-loved isle.

O Thou ! who poured the patriotic tide
    That streamed thro' Wallace's undaunted heart,
Who dared to nobly stem tyrannic pride,
    Or nobly die—the second glorious part,
    (The patriot's God, peculiarly thou art
His friend, inspirer, guardian, and reward !)
    O never, never, Scotia's realm desert ;
But still the patriot, and the patriot-bard,
In bright succession rise, her ornament and guard !

TAM O' SHANTER

When chapman billies leave the street,
And drouthy neibors neibors meet,
As market-days are wearing late,
An' folk begin to tak the gate ;
While we sit bousing at the nappy,
An' getting fou and unco happy,
We think na on the lang Scots miles,
The mosses, waters, slaps, and styles,
That lie between us and our hame,
Where sits our sulky sullen dame,
Gathering her brows like gathering storm,
Nursing her wrath to keep it warm.
    This truth fand honest Tam o' Shanter,
As he frae Ayr ae night did canter—
(Auld Ayr, wham ne'er a town surpasses
For honest men and bonnie lasses).
    O Tam ! hadst thou but been sae wise
As ta'en thy ain wife Kate's advice !
She tauld thee weel thou was a skellum,
A bletherin', blusterin', drunken blellum ;
That frae November till October,
Ae market-day thou was na sober ;
That ilka melder wi' the miller
Thou sat as lang as thou had siller ;
That every naig was ca'd a shoe on,
The smith and thee gat roarin' fou on ;
That at the Lord's house, even on Sunday,
Thou drank wi' Kirkton Jean till Monday.
She prophesied that, late or soon,
Thou would be found deep drown'd in Doon ;

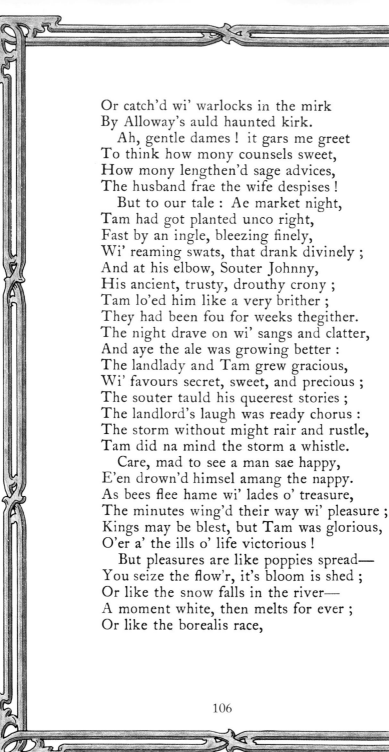

Or catch'd wi' warlocks in the mirk
By Alloway's auld haunted kirk.

   Ah, gentle dames ! it gars me greet
To think how mony counsels sweet,
How mony lengthen'd sage advices,
The husband frae the wife despises !

   But to our tale : Ae market night,
Tam had got planted unco right,
Fast by an ingle, bleezing finely,
Wi' reaming swats, that drank divinely ;
And at his elbow, Souter Johnny,
His ancient, trusty, drouthy crony ;
Tam lo'ed him like a very brither ;
They had been fou for weeks thegither.
The night drave on wi' sangs and clatter,
And aye the ale was growing better :
The landlady and Tam grew gracious,
Wi' favours secret, sweet, and precious ;
The souter tauld his queerest stories ;
The landlord's laugh was ready chorus :
The storm without might rair and rustle,
Tam did na mind the storm a whistle.

   Care, mad to see a man sae happy,
E'en drown'd himsel amang the nappy.
As bees flee hame wi' lades o' treasure,
The minutes wing'd their way wi' pleasure ;
Kings may be blest, but Tam was glorious,
O'er a' the ills o' life victorious !

   But pleasures are like poppies spread—
You seize the flow'r, it's bloom is shed ;
Or like the snow falls in the river—
A moment white, then melts for ever ;
Or like the borealis race,

That flit ere you can point their place ;
Or like the rainbow's lovely form
Evanishing amid the storm.
Nae man can tether time nor tide ;
The hour approaches Tam maun ride ;
That hour, o' night's black arch the key-stane,
That dreary hour, he mounts his beast in ;
And sic a night he taks the road in
As ne'er poor sinner was abroad in.
    The wind blew as 'twad blawn its last ;
The rattling show'rs rose on the blast ;
The speedy gleams the darkness swallow'd ;
Loud, deep, and lang, the thunder bellow'd :
That night, a child might understand,
The Deil had business on his hand.
    Weel mounted on his gray mare, Meg,
A better never lifted leg,
Tam skelpit on thro' dub and mire,
Despising wind, and rain, and fire ;
Whiles holding fast his gude blue bonnet ;
Whiles crooning o'er some auld Scots sonnet ;
Whiles glow'ring round wi' prudent cares,
Lest bogles catch him unawares.
Kirk-Alloway was drawing nigh,
Whare ghaists and houlets nightly cry.
    By this time he was cross the ford,
Where in the snaw the chapman smoor'd ;
And past the birks and meikle stane,
Where drunken Charlie brak's neck-bane ;
And thro' the whins, and by the cairn,
Where hunters fand the murder'd bairn ;
And near the thorn, aboon the well,
Where Mungo's mither hang'd hersel.

Before him Doon pours all his floods ;
The doubling storm roars thro' the woods ;
The lightnings flash from pole to pole ;
Near and more near the thunders roll :
When, glimmering thro' the groaning trees,
Kirk-Alloway seem'd in a bleeze ;
Thro' ilka bore the beams were glancing ;
And loud resounded mirth and dancing.
   Inspiring bold John Barleycorn !
What dangers thou canst make us scorn !
Wi' tippenny, we fear nae evil ;
Wi' usquebae, we'll face the devil !
The swats sae ream'd in Tammie's noddle,
Fair play, he car'd na deils a boddle !
But Maggie stood right sair astonish'd,
Till, by the heel and hand admonish'd,
She ventur'd forward on the light ;
And, vow ! Tam saw an unco sight !
Warlocks and witches in a dance !
Nae cotillon brent new frae France,
But hornpipes, jigs, strathspeys, and reels,
Put life and mettle in their heels.
A winnock-bunker in the east,
There sat auld Nick, in shape o' beast—
A touzie tyke, black, grim, and large !
To gie them music was his charge :
He screw'd the pipes and gart them skirl,
Till roof and rafters a' did dirl.
Coffins stood round like open presses,
That shaw'd the dead in their last dresses ;
And by some devilish cantraip sleight
Each in its cauld hand held a light,
By which heroic Tam was able

To note upon the haly table
A murderer's banes in gibbet-airns ;
Twa span-lang, wee, unchristen'd bairns ;
A thief new-cutted frae the rape—
Wi' his last gasp his gab did gape ;
Five tomahawks, wi' blude red rusted ;
Five scymitars, wi' murder crusted ;
A garter, which a babe had strangled ;
A knife, a father's throat had mangled,
Whom his ain son o' life bereft—
The gray hairs yet stack to the heft ;
Wi' mair of horrible and awfu',
Which even to name wad be unlawfu'.

    As Tammie glowr'd, amaz'd, and curious,
The mirth and fun grew fast and furious :
The piper loud and louder blew ;
The dancers quick and quicker flew ;
They reel'd, they set, they cross'd, they cleekit,
Till ilka carlin swat and reekit,
And coost her duddies to the wark,
And linkit at it in her sark !

    Now Tam, O Tam ! had thae been queans,
A' plump and strapping in their teens ;
Their sarks, instead o' creeshie flannen,
Been snaw-white seventeen hunder linen !
Thir breeks o' mine, my only pair,
That ance were plush, o' gude blue hair,
I wad hae gi'en them off my hurdies,
For ae blink o' the bonnie burdies !

    But wither'd beldams, auld and droll,
Rigwoodie hags wad spean a foal,
Louping and flinging on a crummock,
I wonder didna turn thy stomach.

But Tam kent what was what fu' brawlie :
There was ae winsome wench and walie
That night enlisted in the core,
Lang after kent on Carrick shore !
(For mony a beast to dead she shot,
And perish'd mony a bonnie boat,
And shook baith meikle corn and bear,
And kept the country-side in fear.)
Her cutty sark, o' Paisley harn,
That while a lassie she had worn,
In longitude tho' sorely scanty,
It was her best, and she was vauntie.
Ah ! little kent thy reverend grannie
That sark she coft for her wee Nannie
Wi' twa pund Scots ('twas a' her riches)
Wad ever grac'd a dance of witches !
　　But here my muse her wing maun cour ;
Sic flights are far beyond her pow'r—
To sing how Nannie lap and flang,
(A souple jad she was, and strang) ;
And how Tam stood, like ane bewitch'd,
And thought his very een enrich'd ;
Even Satan glowr'd, and fidg'd fu' fain,
And hotch'd and blew wi' might and main :
Till first ae caper, syne anither,
Tam tint his reason a' thegither,
And roars out ' Weel done, Cutty-sark ! '
And in an instant all was dark !
And scarcely had he Maggie rallied,
When out the hellish legion sallied.
　　As bees bizz out wi' angry fyke
When plundering herds assail their byke,
As open pussie's mortal foes

When pop ! she starts before their nose,
As eager runs the market-crowd,
When 'Catch the thief !' resounds aloud.
So Maggie runs ; the witches follow,
Wi' mony an eldritch skriech and hollow.
 Ah, Tam ! ah, Tam ! thou 'll get thy fairin' !
In hell they'll roast thee like a herrin' !
In vain thy Kate awaits thy comin' !
Kate soon will be a woefu' woman !
Now do thy speedy utmost, Meg,
And win the key-stane o' the brig :
There at them thou thy tail may toss,
A running stream they dare na cross !
But ere the key-stane she could make,
The fient a tail she had to shake :
For Nannie, far before the rest,
Hard upon noble Maggie prest,
And flew at Tam wi' furious ettle ;
But little wist she Maggie's mettle !
Ae spring brought off her master hale,
But left behind her ain gray tail :
The carlin claught her by the rump,
And left poor Maggie scarce a stump.
 Now, wha this tale o' truth shall read,
Each man and mother's son, take heed ;
Whene'er to drink you are inclin'd,
Or cutty-sarks rin in your mind,
Think ! ye may buy the joys o'er dear ;
Remember Tom o' Shanter's mare.

THE VISION

THE sun had closed the winter day,
The curlers quat their roarin' play,
An' hunger'd maukin taen her way
      To kail-yards green,
While faithless snaws ilk step betray
      Where she has been.

The thresher's weary flingin'-tree
The lee-lang day had tirèd me :
And when the day had clos'd his e'e,
      Far i' the west,
Ben i' the spence, right pensivelie,
      I gaed to rest.

There lanely by the ingle-cheek
I sat and eyed the spewing reek,
That fill'd, wi' hoast-provoking smeek,
      The auld clay biggin' ;
An' heard the restless rattons squeak
      About the riggin'.

All in this mottie misty clime,
I backward mused on wasted time,
How I had spent my youthfu' prime,
      An' done nae-thing,
But stringin' blethers up in rhyme,
      For fools to sing.

Had I to guid advice but harkit,
I might, by this, hae led a market,
Or strutted in a bank, and clarkit
      My cash-account :
While here, half-mad, half-fed, half-sarkit,
        Is a' th' amount.

I started, mutt'ring 'blockhead ! coof !'
And heaved on high my waukit loof,
To swear by a' yon starry roof,
      Or some rash aith,
That I, henceforth, would be rhyme-proof
        Till my last breath—

When click ! the string the snick did draw ;
An' jee ! the door gaed to the wa' ;
And by my ingle-lowe I saw,
      Now bleezin' bright,
A tight outlandish hizzie, braw,
        Come full in sight.

Ye need na doubt I held my whisht ;
The infant aith, half-form'd, was crusht ;
I glowr'd as eerie's I'd been dusht
      In some wild glen ;
When sweet, like modest worth, she blusht,
        An' steppèd ben.

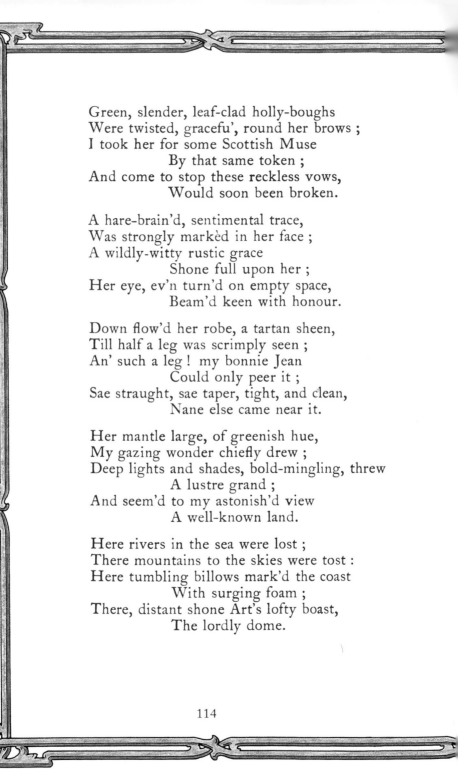

Green, slender, leaf-clad holly-boughs
Were twisted, gracefu', round her brows ;
I took her for some Scottish Muse
   By that same token ;
And come to stop these reckless vows,
   Would soon been broken.

A hare-brain'd, sentimental trace,
Was strongly markèd in her face ;
A wildly-witty rustic grace
   Shone full upon her ;
Her eye, ev'n turn'd on empty space,
   Beam'd keen with honour.

Down flow'd her robe, a tartan sheen,
Till half a leg was scrimply seen ;
An' such a leg ! my bonnie Jean
   Could only peer it ;
Sae straught, sae taper, tight, and clean,
   Nane else came near it.

Her mantle large, of greenish hue,
My gazing wonder chiefly drew ;
Deep lights and shades, bold-mingling, threw
   A lustre grand ;
And seem'd to my astonish'd view
   A well-known land.

Here rivers in the sea were lost ;
There mountains to the skies were tost :
Here tumbling billows mark'd the coast
   With surging foam ;
There, distant shone Art's lofty boast,
   The lordly dome.

Here Doon pour'd down his far-fetch'd floods ;
There well-fed Irwine stately thuds ;
Auld hermit Ayr staw thro' his woods,
      On to the shore ;
And many a lesser torrent scuds,
      With seeming roar.

Low in a sandy valley spread,
An ancient borough rear'd her head ;
Still, as in Scottish story read,
      She boasts a race
To ev'ry nobler virtue bred,
      And polish'd grace.

By stately tower or palace fair,
Or ruins pendent in the air,
Bold stems of heroes, here and there,
      I could discern ;
Some seem'd to muse, some seem'd to dare,
      With feature stern.

My heart did glowing transport feel,
To see a race heroic wheel,
And brandish round the deep-dyed steel
      In sturdy blows ;
While back-recoiling seem'd to reel
      Their Suthron foes.

His Country's Saviour, mark him well !
Bold Richardton's heroic swell ;
The Chief—on Sark who glorious fell,
      In high command ;
And he whom ruthless fates expel
      His native land.

There, where a sceptred Pictish shade
Stalk'd round his ashes lowly laid,
I mark'd a martial race, pourtray'd
            In colours strong ;
Bold, soldier-featured, undismay'd
            They strode along.

DUAN SECOND

With musing-deep astonish'd stare,
I view'd the heavenly-seeming Fair ;
A whisp'ring throb did witness bear
            Of kindred sweet,
When with an elder Sister's air
            She did me greet.

' All hail ! my own inspired bard !
In me thy native Muse regard !
Nor longer mourn thy fate is hard,
            Thus poorly low ;
I come to give thee such reward
            As we bestow.

' Know, the great Genius of this land
Has many a light aërial band,
Who, all beneath his high command,
            Harmoniously,
As arts or arms they understand,
            Their labours ply.

' They Scotia's race among them share :
Some fire the soldier on to dare ;
Some rouse the patriot up to bare
            Corruption's heart :
Some teach the bard, a darling care,
            The tuneful art.

'Of these am I—Coila my name;
And this district as mine I claim,
Where once the Campbells, chiefs of fame,
        Held ruling pow'r:
I mark'd thy embryo-tuneful flame,
        Thy natal hour.

'With future hope I oft would gaze,
Fond, on thy little early ways,
Thy rudely-caroll'd, chiming phrase,
        In uncouth rhymes,—
Fired at the simple artless lays
        Of other times.

'I saw thee seek the sounding shore,
Delighted with the dashing roar;
Or when the North his fleecy store
        Drove thro' the sky,
I saw grim Nature's visage hoar
        Struck thy young eye.

'Or when the deep green-mantled Earth
Warm-cherish'd ev'ry flow'ret's birth,
And joy and music pouring forth
        In ev'ry grove,
I saw thee eye the gen'ral mirth
        With boundless love.

'When ripen'd fields and azure skies
Call'd forth the reapers' rustling noise,
I saw thee leave their ev'ning joys,
        And lonely stalk,
To vent thy bosom's swelling rise
        In pensive walk.

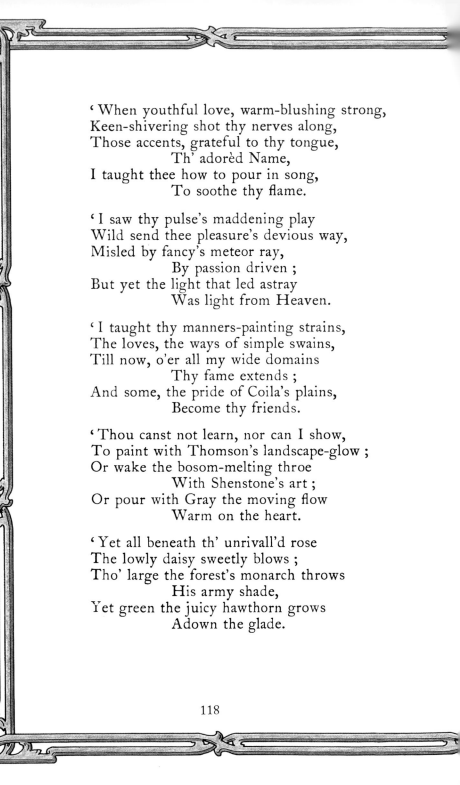

'When youthful love, warm-blushing strong,
Keen-shivering shot thy nerves along,
Those accents, grateful to thy tongue,
    Th' adorèd Name,
I taught thee how to pour in song,
    To soothe thy flame.

'I saw thy pulse's maddening play
Wild send thee pleasure's devious way,
Misled by fancy's meteor ray,
    By passion driven ;
But yet the light that led astray
    Was light from Heaven.

'I taught thy manners-painting strains,
The loves, the ways of simple swains,
Till now, o'er all my wide domains
    Thy fame extends ;
And some, the pride of Coila's plains,
    Become thy friends.

'Thou canst not learn, nor can I show,
To paint with Thomson's landscape-glow ;
Or wake the bosom-melting throe
    With Shenstone's art ;
Or pour with Gray the moving flow
    Warm on the heart.

'Yet all beneath th' unrivall'd rose
The lowly daisy sweetly blows ;
Tho' large the forest's monarch throws
    His army shade,
Yet green the juicy hawthorn grows
    Adown the glade.

'Then never murmur nor repine;
Strive in thy humble sphere to shine;
And trust me, not Potosi's mine,
              Nor king's regard,
Can give a bliss o'ermatching thine,
              A rustic Bard.

'To give my counsels all in one,
Thy tuneful flame still careful fan;
Preserve the dignity of Man,
              With Soul erect;
And trust the Universal Plan
              Will all protect.

'And wear thou this': She solemn said,
And bound the holly round my head:
The polish'd leaves and berries red
              Did rustling play;
And, like a passing thought, she fled
              In light away.

AULD LANG SYNE

SHOULD auld acquaintance be forgot,
  And never brought to min' ?
Should auld acquaintance be forgot,
  And auld lang syne ?

    For auld lang syne, my dear.
      For auld lang syne,
    We 'll tak a cup o' kindness yet,
      For auld lang syne.

We twa hae run about the braes,
  And pu'd the gowans fine ;
But we 've wander'd mony a weary foot
  Sin' auld lang syne.

We twa hae paidled i' the burn,
  From morning sun till dine ;
But seas between us braid hae roar'd
  Sin' auld lang syne.

And there 's a hand, my trusty fiere,
  And gie 's a hand o' thine ;
And we 'll tak a right guid-willie waught,
  For auld lang syne.

And surely ye 'll be your pint-stowp,
  And surely I 'll be mine ;
And we 'll tak a cup o' kindness yet
  For auld lang syne.

    For auld lang syne, my dear.
      For auld lang syne,
    We 'll tak a cup o' kindness yet,
      For auld lang syne.

Glossary

Abeigh, aloof, at bay.
Aboon, above.
Acquent, acquainted.
Ae, one; only.
Aff-loof, offhand.
A-gley, askew.
Aiblins, perhaps, possibly.
Airt, region, direction; to direct.
Airted, directed.
Aizle, ash (of fuel); a cinder.
Ajee, ajar.
An, if.
Asklent, askance.
Ava, at all; of all.
Awnie, bearded (barley).
Ayont, beyond.

Babie-clouts, baby-clothes.
Bairntime, a mother's whole brood or issue.
Bade, endured, could stand.
Bannock, a soft flat cake.
Barley - bree, barley - brew = ale or whisky.
Baudrons, the cat.
Bawsent, white streaked.
Beets, adds fuel to, incites.
Bell, flower, blossom; **sin' lint was i' the bell,** since flax was in blossom.
Belyve, by and by, presently.
Ben, the spence or parlour; in, into, the inner room.
Beuk, a book.
Bicker, a wooden cup; a draught.
Bickering, hurrying.
Biel, bield, a shelter.
Bien, comfortable.
Big, to build.
Biggin, a building.
Bill, a bull.

Billie, brother; comrade.
Bings, heaps.
Birk, a birch (tree).
Birkie, chap, fellow (carries a suggestion of strut, conceit or cockiness).
Birken-shaw, a wood of birches.
Bizz, to buzz.
Blate, bashful, shy.
Blaud, a slapping lot.
Blellum, a gassy fool.
Blethers, nonsense.
Blink, to glance brightly; a glance; a moment.
Blinkers, spies.
Bluntie, stupid, like a fool.
Bocked, vomited.
Boddle, a small coin, about = $\frac{1}{2}$d.
Bogle, a ghost.
Boortrees, elder-bushes.
Bore, a hole or gap.
Boot, more than they bargained for.
Bouk, a bulk, body.
Braing't, pulled with a jerk.
Brak's, broke his.
Branks, a wooden curb, a bridle.
Brats, clothes; aprons.
Brattle, a spurt, sprint, scamper.
Braw, handsome; gaily dressed.
Braxies, sheep that have died of braxy.
Briestit, sprang forward.
Brechan, a horse-collar.
Brent, smooth, upright.
Brent-new, brand-new.
Brock, a badger.
Brogue, a trick.
Broo, brew, liquid, water.
Broozes, wedding-races home from church.
Brugh, a borough.
Brulzie, a brawl or brangle.

Brunstane, brimstone.
Bughtin, gathering sheep into the fold or bught.
Buirdly, burly, stalwart.
Bum, to hum.
Bum-clock, the beetle.
Burdies (dim of **burd**), damsels.
Bure, did bear.
Burn, a stream.
Burnewin, the blacksmith.
Bur-thistle, the spear-thistle.
But, without.
But an' ben, the kitchen and parlour.
By, a great deal (" I carena by ").
Byke, a hive ; a crowd.
Byre, a cowshed.

Ca', call; drive (cattle, nails, etc.); push.
Cadger, a hawker.
Caff, chaff.
Caird, a tinker.
Cairn, a (memorial) heap of stones.
Caller, fresh.
Cannie, quiet, gentle, kind (also adv.).
Cantie, merry, jolly.
Cantraip, cantrip, magic, witching.
Carl, an old man.
Carl-hemp, male-hemp.
Carlin, a middle-aged or old woman.
Cast out, quarrel.
Caups, wooden cups.
Chanter, the playing pipe of the bag-pipes.
Chaup, a stroke, a blow.
Chiel, chap, young fellow (eulogistic term).
Chimla, chimney.
Chitter, to shiver.
Claivers, clavers, talk, about anything and nothing.
Clash, gossip, tittle-tattle ; to talk so.
Claught, clutched.
Claut, a handful, a quantity.
Cleed, to clothe.
Cleekit, linked (their arms in dancing).
Clink, money.
Clishmaclaver, palaver.
Cloot, a hoof.
Clud, a cloud.
Coble, a small boat.

Coft, bought.
Cogs, various wooden vessels for food and drink are so called.
Coggie, dim. of **cog.**
Coila, Kyle, a division of Ayrshire.
Coof, cuif, a dolt, ninny ; a mean-spirited fellow.
Coost, did cast.
Cootie, leg-plumed ; a small pail.
Corbies, crows.
Couthie, kindly, comfortable.
Cour, to cower.
Crack, a story ; a chat.
Crackin, conversing.
Craig (dim. **craigie**), the throat.
Craiks, landrails.
Crambo-clink, rhyme.
Crambo-jingle, rhyming.
Cranreuch, hoar frost.
Crap, a crop.
Creel, an osier basket.
Creepie-chair, stool of repentance.
Creeshie, greasy.
Crood, to coo.
Crouse, confident, bold.
Crowdie, oatmeal and water or milk (=uncooked porridge).
Crummock, a hooked stick.
Cushat, the wood-pigeon.
Cutty, short.

Daffin, funning, skylarking.
Daimen-icker, an ear or two of corn.
Darg, work.
Daw, to dawn.
Dawtit, petted, made much of.
Dead, death.
Deave, deafen.
Diddle, to jog to and fro.
Dight, to winnow or sift ; to wipe.
Din, dun coloured.
Dink, dainty, trim.
Ding, to overthrow, beat.
Dirl, to vibrate, thrill.
Dizzen, a dozen.
Doited, muddled ; bewildered.
Donsie, restive ; wayward.
Doo, a pigeon.
Dooked, ducked.
Dool, sorrow.

Douce, sedate, serious ; seemly.
Dour, stubborn.
Dow, can ; **downa,** cannot.
Dowff, dull.
Dowie, low-spirited, dull, jaded.
Downa bide, cannot stand (them).
Doylt, stupified.
Draigl't, draggled.
Dreigh, tedious, slow, tiresome.
Droop-rump'lt, short-rumped.
Droukit, soaked.
Drouthy, thirsty.
Drucken, drunken.
Drumlie, muddy.
Drumossie Moor, Culloden Field.
Dub, a puddle.
Duds, duddies, clothes.
Duddie, ragged.
Dundee, a Scotch psalm tune.
Dunts, knocks.
Dusht, touched.

Earn, an eagle.
Eerie, apprehensive, frightened, "queer."
Eild, old age, eld.
Elbuck, elbow.
Eldritch, unearthly, fearsome.
Elgin, a Scotch psalm tune.
Erse, Gaelic.
Ettle, intention.
Eydent, diligent.

Fa', to fall ; lot ; to have (by lot) ; to claim.
Faikit, let off, excused.
Fain, fond, glad ; **fain o' ither,** fond of each other.
Fairin, a gift from the Fair : ironically = a thrashing.
Fan', fand, found.
Fash, to mind, trouble oneself.
Fasten-een, Fasten-even (evening before Lent).
Faught, a fight.
Fauldin'-slap, gate of the fold.
Fawsont, seemly, well-doing.
Fecht, a fight.
Feckless, feeble, fit for nothing.
Fell, sharp, tasty.

Fen', fend, a shift or provision ; to provide for, look after.
Ferlie, to wonder.
Fetch't, stopped suddenly.
Fey, fated to death.
Fidge, to fidget.
Fidgin-fain, fidgeting with fainness.
Fiel, well.
Fient, fiend. **The fient a,** devil a . . .
Fiere, comrade.
Fissle, to bustle, be all alive.
Fittie-lan', the hindmost near horse in ploughing.
Fleech'd, beseeched, wheedled.
Flee, a fly.
Fleg, a fright.
Fley'd, frightened, scared.
Flichterin', fluttering.
Flingin-tree, a flail.
Fliskit, fretted and capered.
Foor, fared, went.
Forbye, besides.
Forfairn, worn out.
Forfoughten, exhausted by the conflict.
Forjesket, "jaded with fatigue," R. B.
Fou, full ; drunk.
Foughten, troubled, wearied.
Fyke, fidget.
Fyle, to dirty.

Gae, gave.
Gae, gaed, go, went.
Gairs, slashes (of a stuffed gown).
Gar (pf. **gar'd, gart**) make, cause to.
Gate, gait, the road ; the way ; **a' to the gate,** away, out of the way ; **tak the gate,** start for home.
Gaucie, gawcie, ample, flowing.
Gaun, going.
Geck, to toss the head.
Get, the begettings, offspring.
Genty, trim, elegant.
Geordie, the yellow lettered, a guinea.
Gin, if ; when.
Girn, to twist the face, in chagrin or malice.
Gizz, a wig.
Glaikit, silly, thoughtless.
Glaum'd, clutched.
Gleib, a portion (of land).

123

Glowrin, staring.

Glunch, a scowl.

Gowan, the daisy.

Gowk, a fool ; a guy.

Graith, the implements of an occupation.

Grat, wept.

Gree, a prize ; **bure the gree** = won the victory.

Greet, to weep.

Groanin' maut, the gossips' ale at a lying-in.

Gruntle, the face, phiz.

Grunzie, the phiz (rather, mouth and nose).

Grushie, sturdy-growing.

Guid-father, father-in-law.

Guid-willie, hearty, with good-will.

Gumlie, muddy.

Gusty, tasty.

Hae, have.

Haet (=have it), component term in phrases ; **deil-haet, fient-haet** = devil a bit, devil a one.

Haffets, the temples.

Hafflins, half-like, partly.

Haggis, "A special Scotch pudding made of sheep's entrails, onions, and oatmeal, boiled in a sheep's stomach. The *pièce de résistance* at Burns' Club Dinners, and an esteemed antidote to whisky." Thus Henley and Henderson, with obvious envy.

Hain, to use sparingly ; be out of use.

Hairst, har'st, harvest.

Haith, faith !

Haivers, nonsense ; idle chat.

Hal', hald, a holding.

Hallen, a partition wall ; a porch.

Halloween, All Saints' Eve (Oct. 31).

Hammers, blockheads.

Hangie, hangman (nickname for Old Nick).

Hansel, the first gift or getting, supposed to bring luck to the receiver or occasion.

Hap, any warm wrap or covering.

Happer, the hopper of a mill.

Harn, coarse cloth.

Hash, an oaf, dunderhead.

Haslock, the finest of the wool.

Haud, to hold.

Haughs, low-lying rich lands.

Hauns, hands.

Havins, manners, conduct.

Hawkie, the cow.

Hech, dear me ! (expression of surprise and grief).

Heft, a haft, handle.

Heigh, high.

Hein-shinned, crooked shinned.

Herriment, plundering, devastation.

Heugh, a hollow or pit.

Hilch, to hobble, halt.

Hiltie-skiltie, helter-skelter.

Hirples, limps.

Histie, bare.

Hizzie, a wench, young woman.

Hoast, a cough.

Hog-shouther, shouldering, jostling.

Hoolie ! beware !

Houlet, an owl.

Howdie, midwife

Howe, a hollow.

Howket, they dug ; dug up, unearthed.

Hoyte, "to amble crazily," R.B.

Hughoc = little Hugh.

Hunkers, the hams.

Hurdies, the buttocks.

Hushion, a footless stocking, worn on the arm.

Icker, an ear of corn.

Ilka, each, every.

Indentin', indenturing, devoting.

Ingine, genius.

I'se, I will or shall.

Ither, other, another, each other.

Jad, a jade.

Jauk, to trifle, dally.

Jaups, splashes.

Jimp, small, slender.

Jimps, stays.

Jink, to dodge, to turn quickly this way and that.

Jinker, a spanker ; a coquette.

Jirkinet, bodice.

Jirt, a jerk.

Jo, sweetheart.
Jouk, to duck down, cower.
Jundie, to justle.

Kain, farm produce paid as rent.
Kebars, rafters.
Kebbuck, a cheese.
Keek, peep.
Kelpies, water-demons.
Kennin, a little, **a** thought (astray, etc.).
Kep, to catch (a ball, etc.).
Ket, a fleece.
Kiaugh, cark, anxiety.
Kilbaigie, an esteemed whisky.
Kimmer, wench, gossip, lass (married or single).
Kirn, a churn.
Kirns, harvest-homes.
Kirsen, to christen.
Kist, a chest.
Kitchen, a relish, treat or extra; to impart a relish to.
Kittle, risky, difficult.
Knaggie, knobbly.
Knap, to break (stones for road-metal).
Knowe, a knoll.
Kyles, skittles.
Kytes, bellies.

Laigh, low.
Laik, lack.
Lairing, sinking in moss or mud.
Laithfu', lothe, bashful.
Lallan, Lowland.
Lane, lone, alone (is used with possessive pronoun: "thou art no thy lane"=not alone).
Lap, leapt.
Lave, the remainder; the rest of them.
Lawin, the reckoning.
Lea (also **lay** and **ley**), untilled or meadow-land
Lea-riz, a strip of grass-land.
Lear, lore, learning.
Lee-lang, livelong.
Leeze me on, a blessing on.
Licket, licked, thrashed.
Lift, the sky; a load, share.
Limmer, a jade.

Lin (also **Linn**), a waterfall.
Link, to go dancingly, trippingly on.
Linkit at it, went at it.
Linties (or **Lintwhites**), linnets.
Loan, a lane.
Loof, palm of the hand; the hand.
Loot, let (past tense).
Lough, a loch, lake.
Loup (also **lowp**), to leap.
Lowe, a flame.
Lug, ear.
Lugget, eared; **lugget caup,** the two-eared cup
Luggie, a **cog** with an upright handle.
Luntin, smoking.
Lyart, faded, blanched.

Mae, more.
Mailin, a farm.
Mark, an old Scots coin (1s. 1½d. stg.).
Martyrs, a Scotch psalm tune.
Maukin, a hare.
Maun, must.
Maut, malt.
Mavis, the thrush.
Melder, a milling, or quantity of corn sent to be ground.
Mell, to meddle.
Mense, good manners, discretion.
Messan, a mongrel.
Midden, a dungheap.
Midden-creels, dungheap baskets.
Mind, to remind; to remember.
Minnie, mother.
Mirk, dark.
Moop, to nibble; to herd with.
Mottie, dusty.
Mou', the mouth.
Moudiewort, a mole.
Muslin-kail, meatless broth.
Mutchkin, a liquid measure=1 pint English.

Naigie, dim. of **naig,** a nag.
Nappy, ale, liquor.
Near-hand, nearly.
Neuk, corner.
New-ca'd, newly driven.
Nieve, fist.

Niffer, exchange.
Nit, a nut.
Nowte, cattle.

Ourie, shivering, drooping.
Out-owre, out-over, away across.
Owsen, oxen.

Pack and thick, confidental.
Paidle, to wade.
Painch, the paunch.
Paitrick, a partridge.
Parishen, the people of a parish.
Pat, did put.
Pattle, a plough-spade.
Paughty, pompous, haughty.
Paukie (or pawkie), sly.
Pechan, the stomach.
Pechin', cramming.
Pint (Scots), two English quarts.
Plack, a small coin, about ½d.
Plaiden, of coarse woollen cloth.
Poind, distrain.
Poortith, poverty.
Poussie, the hare.
Pow, the poll, head.
Pownie, a pony.
Prief, proof.
Priggin', haggling.
Proveses, provosts.
Pyke, to pick.
Pyles, grains, particles.

Quat, quitted.
Quean, a young woman, lass.

Ragweed, the ragwort.
Rair, to roar.
Raize, to excite, to anger.
Ramfeezl'd, fagged out.
Ram-stam, headlong, reckless.
Rant, to rollick, royster.
Rants, jollifications; rows.
Rape, a rope.
Raploch, coarse cloth.
Rash, a rush.
Rash-buss, a clump of rushes.
Ratton, a rat.
Raw, a row (of pins).

Rax, to stretch; to reach. **Rax thy leather,** stretch or exercise thyself.
Reave, to rob. **Red-wat-shod,** red-wet-shod.
Reek, smoke; to smoke.
Reekit, smoked, smoky. **Remead,** remedy.
Rig, a ridge.
Riggin, the roof, roof-tree.
Reestit, scorched; rested = refused to go.
Rigwoodie hags, gallows hags (rigging for the **woodie**).
Rip, (or ripp,) a handful of corn from the sheaf.
Rive, to strain, rend, tear.
Rock, a distaff.
Rockin, a social meeting for song and chat and story, to which the women brought their **rock** or distaff.
Roose, to praise, flatter.
Rowe, to roll.
Rowte, to low, bellow.
Rowth, abundance. **Rung,** a cudgel.

Sair, sore; to serve.
Sarkit, shirted.
Saugh, the willow; **saugh-woodies,** willow-wands.
Sawmont, salmon.
Scaith, hurt.
Scar (or Scaur), a jutting cliff, or bank of earth.
Scaur, to scare; (adj.) readily scared.
Scaud, scald.
Scho, she.
Sconner, to loathe.
Screed, a rent, tear.
Scrievin', careering; tearing along.
Seizins, freehold properties.
Sets you, becomes you.
Seventeen-hunder linen, fine linen, woven in a reed of 1700 divisions.
Shachl't, large and shapeless.
Shavie, a trick.
Shaw, a wood.
Sheuch, a ditch, watercourse.
Shiel, a shed or hut.
Shill, shrill, shrilly. **Sic,** such.
Siller, silver; money; wealth.
Sinsyne, since then.

126